CHINA'S TANG DYNASTY

*W*ith special thanks to Anita Siu of the
Department of Asian Art, The Metropolitan Museum of Art, New York City,
for her invaluable assistance and expert advice.

CHINA'S
TANG
DYNASTY

HEATHER MILLAR

BENCHMARK BOOKS

MARSHALL CAVENDISH
NEW YORK

Benchmark Books
Marshall Cavendish Corporation
99 White Plains Road
Tarrytown, New York 10591-9001

Library of Congress Cataloging-in-Publication Data
Millar, Heather.
   China's Tang dynasty / by Heather Millar.
       p.   cm.— (Cultures of the past)
   Includes bibliographical references and index.
   ISBN 0-7614-0074-5 (vol.)
   1. China—History—T'ang dynasty, 618–907—Juvenile literature. [1. China—History—T'ang dynasty, 618–907.]   I. Title. II. Series.
   DS749.3.M53   1996
   951'.017—dc20   95-6986

SUMMARY: Describes how China under the three-hundred-year rule of the Tang dynasty entered a glittering age of prosperity, conquest, justice, and artistic and literary distinction and includes a time line of Chinese rule from 2000 B.C.E. to the present.

Printed and bound in Italy

Book design by Carol Matsuyama
Photo research by Laurie Platt Winfrey, Carousel Research, Inc.

Front cover: Emperor Tang Tai-cong, "grand ancestor Tang," the founder of the Tang
    dynasty
Back cover: A detail from a late-Tang painting showing the famed army on horseback

Photo Credits
Front cover and pages 6, 8, 21, 34, 50: courtesy Collection of National Palace Museum, Taiwan; back cover and page 7: courtesy of Palace Museum Collection, Taichung; pages 10, 12 *(bottom),* 17, 26, 27, 71: Laurie Platt Winfrey; pages 11, 12 *(top),* 23 *(top),* 23 *(bottom),* 37, 49, 57: E. T. Archive; page 14: Metropolitan Museum of Art. Kennedy Fund, 1913; pages 18, 31, 38, 41: The Granger Collection; page 20: Werner Forman Archive/Idemitsu Museum of Arts, Tokyo; pages 25, 45: Musée Guimet, Paris; page 28: Erich Lessing/Art Resource, NY; page 29: Copyright British Museum; page 30: Giraudon/Art Resource, NY; page 33: Werner Forman Archive/China House of Arts, New York; pages 35, 54: Asian Art Archaeology/Art Resource, NY; page 43: Werner Forman Archive; pages 46, 65: George Chan/Photo Researchers; page 48: Werner Forman Archive/Mr. & Mrs. Myron S. Falk, Jr., New York; page 60: Werner Forman Archive/Yamato Bunkaken, Nara, Japan; page 62: Werner Forman Archive/Christian Deydier, London; page 63: Noboru Komine/Photo Researchers; pages 64, 67: Will & Demi McIntyre/Photo Researchers; page 66: Rick Browne/Photo Researchers; page 68: Pertti Nikkila/Photo Researchers; page 70: Asian Art Museum

CONTENTS

A GLITTERING AGE

The ruling class lived life on a grand scale in the Chinese capital of Chang-an. Though painted during a later dynasty, this palace scene is typical of the Tang court.

There was, quite simply, nothing like it in the world. At its height—around the eighth century C.E.*—the capital of the Tang dynasty was the biggest, grandest, most advanced city in the world. The Chinese emperors called it Chang-an, meaning "Long-Lasting Peace." They built it to be the impressive center of what was then the largest empire on earth, a kingdom that stretched from Persia to the Pacific Ocean.

Someone approaching Chang-an might mistake the suburbs for the city itself. But then the visitor would see the city walls. Covered with gray brick, they towered three stories high, much higher than the height of the average peasant house. One million people lived inside the gates. Counting the suburbs, two million called Chang-an home, more than the number of people who now live in Manhattan! At the time of Chang-an's glory London was just a market town of a few thousand people.

Passing the guards at the main city entrance, the newcomer would enter a planned city of boulevards and luxurious town houses laid out like a checkerboard. A grand avenue led from the main gate across town to the imperial palace. This street was 500 feet (152 meters) wide, almost as broad as two football fields. It ran for five miles (eight kilometers).

In the eighth century most people the world over stayed in their villages. They seldom saw strangers from far away. In Chang-an the visitor would pass people from almost everywhere. Merchants from central Asia, with thick beards not often seen in

*Many systems of dating have been used by different cultures throughout history. This series of books uses B.C.E. (Before Common Era) and C.E. (Common Era) instead of B.C. (Before Christ) and A.D. (Anno Domini) out of respect for the diversity of the world's peoples.

China, sold wine from goatskin bags. Blond women, almost never seen in China, shopped in the marketplaces. Religious pilgrims from Korea and Japan wandered the streets in sandals and gray robes. Performing on the streets magicians and dancers from India and Southeast Asia drew crowds.

Tang power was based on its armies, especially the famed horses from Ferghana in Central Asia. Horses were a passion throughout the dynasty, as this detail from a late-Tang painting shows.

Sipping wine from porcelain bowls, court ladies gather around a low table for a concert in this painting from the late Tang. Notice the dog under the table. Pets like small dogs and birds were, and continue to be, popular in China.

Many times a day, guards in silk uniforms would trot through the crowd, banging brass gongs and clearing a path for an imperial official. The government demanded respect. The official rode in a covered chair carried on poles. As he passed, both foreigners and Tang subjects would bow their heads or fall to their knees.

Continuing on, the visitor would see temples and shrines and churches of all kinds. Song could be heard filtering out of a church of Christians from Syria. Five times a day the call to prayer rang out from the Muslim mosques serving Persian and Arab traders. At Daoist temples Chinese wives burned incense that smelled like soap and flowers. And in the temples built to the Indian savior Buddha, Chinese monks chanted sacred texts.

Settling into the life of Chang-an, the visitor would discover a culture as sophisticated as that in a modern global center like Tokyo, New York, or Paris. He or she would hear about the wonders of the imperial palace: the artificial lakes and gardens, the paintings on silk, and the statues of gold. The emperor delighted in polo, a combination of soccer and croquet played on horseback. The Imperial Court had imported the sport from Persia. The emperor kept forty thousand horses in his stables, both for games and for war. He called his favorite horses "dragon steeds."

Though they didn't play polo, fashionable Chang-an ladies had more freedom than women of later Chinese eras. Some even dressed like men and wandered about the city on their own. Tang women loved horseback riding and wearing foreign hairstyles. They ate foods like western pepper and spinach from fine porcelain plates. They loved tea, only recently a popular drink in China.

A small group of rich and powerful aristocrats ruled this vast Chinese empire, leading luxurious and cultured lives. They attended foreign plays and enjoyed concerts given by Chinese orchestras with hundreds of musicians. They collected paintings of landscapes that would become models for later Chinese art. They discussed poetry and wrote it themselves. They read books printed on paper. This was at a time when most Europeans didn't read, and the manuscripts they had were drawn with quill pens on animal skins.

All of the Chinese world—the physical grandeur and political power, the mix of people and religions, the rich culture of theater, literature, and art—would no doubt overwhelm almost any newcomer. If postcards had existed in the eighth century, even a tourist from a big city might have written home, "The Tang dynasty and the capital Chang-an are amazing. You just wouldn't believe it!"

China Before the Tang

When Chang-an was enjoying these heady days, China had already been around for a long, long time. Its borders changed over the years, but essentially it was centered south of the deserts and grasslands of Mongolia and east of the Tibetan plateau. During the Stone Age, people started farming the most fertile land in this area: between the Yellow River in the north and the Yangtze in the south. By 1576 B.C.E., chariot-riding warriors took control of a large area and created a kingdom. Calling themselves the Shang, they built cities and developed China's earliest form of writing. This society was as distant to the Tang as the times of ancient Athens are to modern Americans.

After the Shang other powerful families, or dynasties, became rulers over large areas of what we now call China. To the west a dynasty called Zhou (joe) came to power about 1027 B.C.E. The Zhou conquered the Shang and built a capital city not far from where the Tang would one day build Chang-an.

But nobles started bickering and trying to set themselves up as kings. The Zhou couldn't hold on to power. By about 700 B.C.E. China had become a land with one culture, or set of beliefs and practices, but it still had many rulers. For the next five hundred years Chinese civilization made many advances. Farmers learned to grow soybeans; the first Chinese laws were written; Confucius and others wrote philosophy that still influences China today. But when the Chinese want to curse someone, they say, "May you live in interesting times." For five hundred years Chinese life was a little too interesting: Minor rulers fought each other for power while the people often starved.

Then in 221 B.C.E. the rulers of Qin (chin), a northeastern kingdom, conquered the rest of China's arguing states. The Qin didn't put up with any arguing. They burned books judged harmful to the government. They executed anyone who dared disagree with them. But the Qin also did many good things. The dynasty standardized Chinese writing, weights, and measures. It built roads and canals. It began to build the now famous Great Wall to keep out invaders from the northern plains of Mongolia and Siberia. The harshness of Qin rule, however, finally pushed the people to rebel.

Only twenty years after the Qin dynasty began its rule, a new dynasty, the Han, came to power, in 202 B.C.E. The Han would rule for more than four hundred years, the longest period of unification in Chinese history. Both dynasties shaped the foundations of Chinese culture. For instance, our English word *China* comes from the word *Qin* (also spelled *Chin*); and even today, the Chinese people refer to themselves as the "Han people," the way we call ourselves Americans.

When the Han dynasty fell in 220 C.E.,

Shang dynasty artists are best known for the figures and utensils they made from bronze. By pouring melted metal into molds, they made figures, bells, bowls, goblets, and many other things. Some bronzes were used for religious purposes. Others, like this elephant, appear to have been created for fun.

it was as devastating as the fall of Rome was in the West. Though people wished for a unified empire, they once again endured chaos as small states battled each other for power. The strife continued for three hundred years until a dynasty named Sui (sway) managed to reunite China in 581. Like the Qin the Sui didn't last very long to enjoy the fruits of their triumph.

This model army, buried with the first Qin emperor, hints at the power of that dynasty. Discovered in 1974, the terra-cotta army still has not been completely uncovered. The soldiers are life-sized and each has different features and clothes.

A Golden Age

That pleasure, and the flowering of a golden age of Chinese culture, fell to the dynasty that followed in 618: the Tang (tong). A man named Li Shi-min (lee shur-meen) prevailed in the free-for-all that followed the collapse of the Sui dynasty. He was a tall, strong man from the northwest. A skilled horseman and warrior, he captured the Sui capital of Chang-an. He ruled under the imperial name Tang Tai-cong (tong tai-tsung); it means "grand ancestor Tang."

Tai-cong sat on the throne for twenty-three years, and China flourished. His armies made conquests in all directions—north to the border with Korea, more than 2,000 miles (3,220 kilometers) west to the dry lands of the Turks, southwest to the mountain kingdom of Tibet, and thousands of miles south to the tropical climes of India and what is now Vietnam. Chinese culture and trade followed the path of military victory. The markets of Chang-an filled to bursting with foreign goods. Nobles from all over Asia came bearing presents to pay tribute to Tang greatness.

Prosperity provided a calm environment in which Chinese government could develop. Tai-cong presided over the writing of a new set of laws that covered crimes such as murder and theft as well as such day-to-day affairs as business agreements. During this

Tang Tai-cong, the dynasty's first emperor, came from mixed Chinese and "barbarian" blood and grew up in northern China. He gained power through prowess in war, as the stone relief (below) shows. The portrait (at right) shows him as a powerful ruler at court.

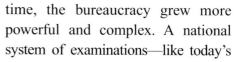

time, the bureaucracy grew more powerful and complex. A national system of examinations—like today's Scholastic Aptitude Tests (SATs), only much more difficult—determined who was chosen for official posts. The examination system was weighted in favor of the rich and powerful, but it was more democratic than early systems of choosing leaders. Even aristocrats had to prove themselves by passing the series of tests given by the imperial government. The structure that was developed during the Tang dynasty worked so well that it survived until the beginning of the twentieth century.

After Tai-cong's death, two ruling personalities dominated the next hundred years. The first was a woman named Wu Chao. She had been one of Tai-cong's concubines, one of many women who were not married to the emperor but lived in his palace and shared his bed when he wanted. Wu Chao won the affection of Tai-cong's son and successor, and gradually eliminated or murdered all of her

THE GOLDEN PEACHES OF SAMARKAND

If a tribal chief or a foreign king or the ruler of a small city wanted to have a relationship with the emperor of Tang China, he had to pay tribute. The Chinese thought that all foreign countries were essentially barbaric. (A bit of that attitude still survives today.) They required foreigners to bring gifts to the imperial court demonstrating that China was superior to all other lands. A modern book called *The Golden Peaches of Samarkand* details the things sent as tribute during the Tang dynasty. A sampling from that book follows:

> Many rulers sent people to serve the court of Tang. Dancing girls came from the ancient kingdom of Iran; musicians from Burma (now called Myanmar) in Southeast Asia. Some nations, like Cambodia, sent whole orchestras as tribute. Slaves captured by victorious Chinese armies were paraded through the streets to the palace.
>
> Rare foods also poured into the palace kitchen. Sixteen butlers handled the influx of such rarities as date palms, perfumed saffron, honeyed bamboo shoots and sugared ginger, dried oysters soaked in wine, summer garlic, deer tongues, Venus clams, sea horses, white carp marinated in wine, melons, cherries, persimmons, and "thorny limes."
>
> Then some messengers brought treasure: tortoise shells for ornaments; yellow amber that the Chinese called "tiger's soul"; hammered gold from Persia, "purple gold"; entire armor suits of silver (which must have been only for show; silver is soft); jade birds decorated with gold and silver; jade sculptures of lions and dragons; crystal drinking cups.
>
> Sometimes the gifts got so extravagant that emperors would refuse them as too "frivolous," or silly. The "brilliant emperor" refused a suit of gold for this reason. But then, with all the other presents people were giving him, the Son of Heaven could afford to say no once in a while.

rivals. Finally she declared herself a reborn goddess and took the throne. She is still the only woman in Chinese history to have ruled in her own name. She was ruthless, but effective. During her reign the Tang civil service grew stronger, and the empire grew larger than ever before. In 705, Wu Chao, then in her eighties, fell victim to plotters in her palace.

After a few years of confusion another strong ruler, Xuan-cang (SHOO-an-sahng), took the throne. His reign came to be considered so important that history has also given him the name Ming Huang (ming who-ahng), meaning "brilliant emperor." Artists, painters, and poets gathered at his court, which was known for its riches.

Unfortunately Xuan-cang may have lived too long for his own good. In his later years he became obsessed with one of his son's concubines, Yang Kui-fei (yong kway-fay). She was so beautiful, the emperor would do anything for her. Soon Yang Kui-fei started to use her relationship with the emperor to get her friends and relatives high government jobs. Her favorite general, a fat witty Turk named An Lu-shan, had the run of the palace as her adopted son. The emperor punished anyone who questioned these changes, something he would not have done earlier in his reign.

As the situation grew worse, General An Lu-shan had a dispute with Yang Kui-fei's brother. In 755 the general led a rebellion that lasted almost eight years. An's forces pillaged cities and attacked the capital. The emperor, his beloved Yang Kui-fei, and his court fled. Palace guards blamed all the empire's troubles on Yang Kui-fei. They strangled her and threw her body in a ditch. The emperor surrendered his throne in shame and sorrow.

Though order eventually returned and culture thrived once again, the Tang government never fully recovered from this blow. Palace servants became very powerful and even murdered two emperors who did not please them. The dynasty had little power outside China proper—the eastern coast and the inland areas between the Yellow and Yangtze Rivers.

Despite these problems, the later Tang rulers improved such

Emperor Xuan-cang helped create the dynasty's second flowering of culture. He created the famous Han Lin Academy, a university for scholars. In this painting, the yellow-robed emperor instructs a prince who sits on a stool.

YANG KUI-FEI—CHINA'S FEMME FATALE

It's not surprising that the Tang emperor Xuan-cang fell in love with the "precious concubine" Yang Kui-fei. The main job of a concubine was to look beautiful and bring pleasure to her master. By all accounts Yang Kui-fei was drop-dead gorgeous by the standards of the times. She was plump; that was considered pretty. She piled her hair up in elaborate hairdos decorated with ornaments, pearls, and combs. She knew how to dance and sing to entertain her master.

If Yang Kui-fei had limited her activities to fashion and dancing, no one would have criticized her. But she used her influence over the emperor to have her friends and relatives given important jobs. Finally a rebellion resulted. Yang Kui-fei was killed. The emperor who adored her gave up his throne. Because of these events Yang Kui-fei forever became a symbol of the evil woman. Sometimes this is called a femme fatale, French for "fatal woman." It refers to the idea that such women destroy their admirers.

Yang Kui-fei and her emperor inspired many stories of Tang times. A famous Tang poet, Po Chu-i (poe choo-EE), wrote a poem about Yang Kui-fei's romance and called it "The Song of Everlasting Sorrow." Later dynasties produced poems, operas, and plays based on the story of the Tang concubine. The tale was even told in Japan. The legend has had lasting appeal. In 1993 Chinese TV broadcast a forty-part series called *Concubine Yang*.

things as the transport of grain to the capital. New taxes kept Chang-an prosperous. Some of the provinces that had been lost during the rebellion came under Tang control again. Emperors

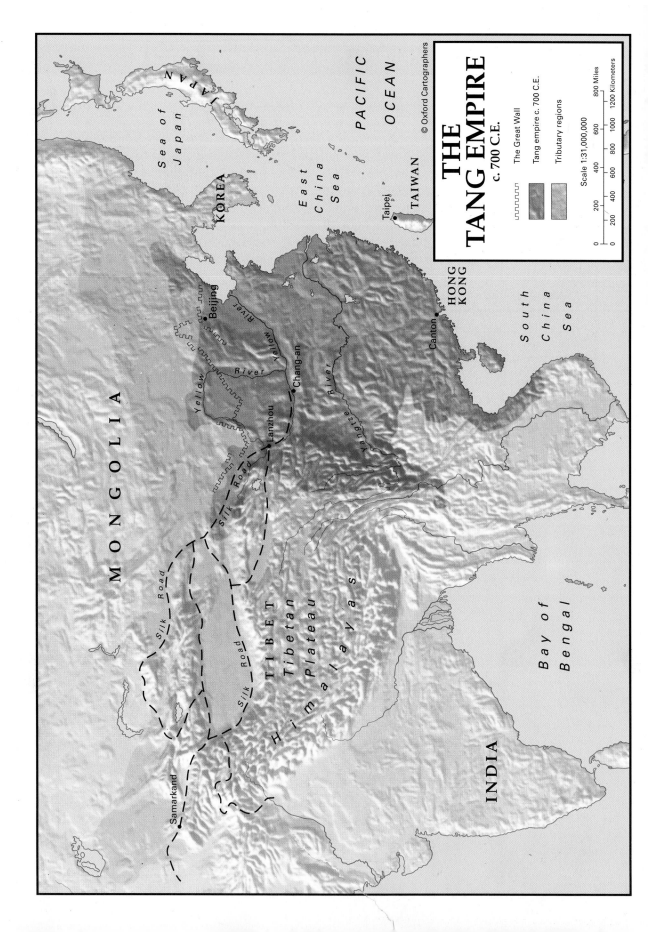

PACIFIC
OCEAN

© Oxford Cartographers

THE
TANG EMPIRE
c. 700 C.E.

The Great Wall

Tang empire c. 700 C.E.

Tributary regions

Scale 1:31,000,000

| 0 | 200 | 400 | 600 | 800 Miles |

| 0 | 200 | 400 | 600 | 800 | 1000 | 1200 Kilometers |

Sea of
Japan

JAPAN

KOREA

East
China
Sea

TAIWAN

Taipei

South
China
Sea

HONG KONG

Canton

Beijing

Yellow River

Yellow River

Chang-an

Lanzhou

Silk Road

Yangtze River

MONGOLIA

Silk Road

Silk Road

Silk Road

TIBET

Tibetan
Plateau

Himalayas

Bay of
Bengal

Samarkand

INDIA

After the An Lu-shan rebellion, the Emperor Xuan-Zang had to flee with his court. His legendary journey to Shu, shown in this anonymous painting, became a common theme for artists.

reasserted imperial power over religious leaders who had grown so powerful that they competed with the court.

But as the years passed, small-scale rebellions, mutinies, and humiliations from provincial governors began to torment the Tang emperors more and more. During the dynasty's last fifty years the government became hopelessly mismanaged. Meanwhile desperately poor and homeless people formed gangs. In Hu-nan, a south-central province stricken by drought and poverty, an uprising of the poor quickly engulfed most of east and central China.

The final fighting devastated once glorious Chang-an. Panic coursed through the streets. People screamed; blood flowed. Severed heads lay on the ground. Once elegant town houses burned. Foxes and rabbits wandered through deserted palaces. Brambles grew in old gardens. The first Han dynasty emperor had made Chang-an his chief city one thousand years before. After the Tang dynasty fell, Chang-an would never again be China's capital.

But its legend lives on to this day.

CHAPTER TWO

OF POEMS AND BAMBOO BRUSHES

The glory of Tang civilization depended on the labors of peasants. This Tang dynasty painting found on the wall of a cave in western China shows farmers plowing and watering a rice field. Notice that they wade in the mud barefoot!

The Chinese like to boast that they are a nation with more than four thousand years of history. The story of their culture spans dynasty after dynasty: works of brilliant writers that modern leaders still study; religious sculptures that tower hundreds of feet high; poems carved into mountain faces in letters twenty feet (six meters) tall; porcelain bowls so delicate that light shines through them; giant construction projects such as the famous Great Wall, the only

man-made object clearly visible from space. Even in this long and fantastic tale, the Tang dynasty stands out.

Many historians say that the Tang dynasty was the turning point between ancient and modern China. When the first Tang emperor took the throne, all the old Chinese traditions were in place. By the time the dynasty fell, the nation's culture had developed the beginnings of all the things we today consider typically Chinese.

Day-to-Day Life

The civilization that gave rise to these wonders was built on a foundation of peasant farmers. Most people lived in the countryside. Their lives were ruled by family, the seasons, and the crops. In some areas the sound of a drum called the workers together and beat out a work rhythm. The drum could be heard from sunrise until dusk. Men toiled in the fields, growing wheat in the north of the country and rice in the south.

Peasant life was hard. Horses and oxen were rare and expensive to feed, so people often pulled the plows. Even a good harvest barely supplied basic needs. Most days, peasants ate beans, rice, and small amounts of vegetables such as turnips or cabbage spiced with soy sauce and garlic. They owned one set of clothes and lived in a one-room house of brick or dirt. Any disaster, such as a war, a failed crop, or a drought, might mean starvation.

Common people knew little of painting or poetry. The cultured world of the capital was far removed from their day-to-day lives. As long as they were left to farm in peace, most didn't think of the emperor very often. They had a saying, "A good place is where the sky is high and the emperor is far." When they thought of the emperor at all, they trusted him to tell the gods to bring good weather and abundant harvests.

"All Under Heaven"

It seemed perfectly normal to think that the emperor could control the weather and make the crops grow. To the Chinese, their ruler wasn't exactly a god, but he was something more than a human. He and his government formed a bridge between heaven and earth.

The emperor's authority came from heaven. The supreme god gave him the right to rule as long as he did so justly and cared for his subjects. The emperor's domain was everything under heaven. Droughts, comets, eclipses, for example, were seen as signs of heaven's displeasure with the emperor. If too many disasters occurred at the same time, it might mean that the ruler had lost the approval of the gods. In such cases the Chinese thought it was their duty to rebel.

Thousands of Servants

Chinese emperors ruled at the top of an enormous household and government. The imperial court included the emperor, his wife, and their children. It also included the emperor's concubines, who lived in his house and had children by him. The concubines lived in a separate part of the palace. Eunuchs (you-nucks) took care of the concubines. They were men who had been castrated and thus could not father children. They could not marry, but they often became very powerful because of their close relationship with the emperor's family. In addition, the court included thousands of officials and servants—from the very grand minister of war down to the servant whose only job was to dust and clean the emperor's curtains.

The emperor, of course, occupied the top spot. He had absolute power. If someone displeased him, he could order him beheaded on the spot. If he was feeling cheery, he could make a man rich with one command. At court everyone was always scheming to get on the emperor's good side or to get competitors in trouble. A lot of the emperor's day was spent coping with these conspiracies, attending parties, and leading ceremonies to ensure that the gods remained happy.

The day-to-day task of running the government fell to the large class of civil servants, or "scholar-officials." Most of these men came from privileged families. But they still had to pass a series of very difficult exams to get their jobs. These were the men who ran the government

At the Tang court, even musicians and servants dressed with style. This figurine, placed in a tomb of the royal family, shows a kneeling female musician holding a flute. Her hair—gathered up into a high bun—would have been very fashionable in Tang times.

monopolies in salt and iron, collected the taxes, made sure roads were built, organized army posts along China's borders, enforced laws, and performed hundreds of other jobs. They also wrote letters with beautiful handwriting, or calligraphy (kuh-LIH-gruh-fee). They composed poetry and painted. They were so skilled in the arts that they created much of what is known today as Chinese culture. They were scholars as well as officials.

Tang scholars often got together to eat, drink, and match wits with one another. A common party game was to compose poetry. In a painting created just after the Tang dynasty, men of letters gather around a banquet table.

What's in a Word?

Words had a central place in this culture, much as the emperor did in the government. The Chinese don't use letters to form words. They write with symbols. We call them characters; the Chinese call them *zi* (zuh). Each character stands for one word, but two or more characters can be combined for more complicated words. Many of these characters started out thousands of years ago as pictures. The character for *mouth* looked like a mouth. The character *to lead* was a picture of a hand holding an elephant trunk. The character for *birth* began as a drawing of a small plant just poking up out of the earth.

Gradually these characters became simplified. They looked less like drawings. They have changed very little in the last two thousand years. As they evolved in form, characters also took on more meanings. In English, for example, *hot* can mean "burning in temperature," "fiery-tasting," "popular," or "good-looking." In Chinese almost every character has several meanings like this. For instance, the character for birth, *sheng* (shung), when used as a verb came to mean "to live," "to give birth to," "to be born." As a noun it could mean "life," "young man," "student." As an adjective it might describe something alive, raw, strange, natural, or lively.

So when a Chinese person reads the character *sheng,* it brings to mind a crowd of images: a sprouting plant, birth, life, giving life, young people, students, and things raw, strange, and lively. The reader chooses the right meaning depending on the topic of the sentence. All these meanings and choices can make Chinese essays difficult to understand, but they are the key to Chinese poetry.

A Poem for Every Occasion

Poetry is difficult because it's not always clear. A poem usually doesn't state its meaning directly. It creates a mood, asks a question, sets a scene. The reader has to fill in the blanks. The Chinese language is perfect for this sort of writing. Each word reminds the reader of many things, the way a song on the radio can remind a listener of a certain time or person. In Chinese each character is a world in a syllable; each line is rich with images and ideas.

So for the Tang people making up word pictures or poems was a favorite pastime. These were often about the sorrow of being homesick, or the beauty of a natural scene. Every educated person was expected to be able to compose poems. People often sent poems to each other instead of letters.

Many famous poets lived during the Tang dynasty. Of these, two writers—Li Po and Du Fu—are considered the greatest poets in all of Chinese history. They both served as officials during the

Li Po was a laughing, good-hearted troublemaker who wrote as much about wine as about anything else. Some say he wrote 20,000 poems. Of these, 1,800 survive.

China's two most beloved poets, Li Po and Du Fu, were both minor officials at the emperor's court. But they could not have been more different.

Li Po (701–763) was the older. His energy seemed to be boundless; he was always busy. A tall man, he could handle a sword with skill. He drank a lot and often. As a result he developed a reputation for getting into bar fights. He didn't care about anyone's rules. He treasured the friendship of dancing girls and hermits as much as the respect of the emperor.

Li Po's poems covered almost every topic under the sun. Sometimes he wrote sad verses about missing home. But no matter how he missed his family, no matter how tough life got, Li Po remained open to joy and beauty. He wrote whole sets of poems dedicated to the pleasures of nature and of wine. In one he exulted, "Forever committed to carefree play, we'll all meet again in the Milky Way!" The story of his death is probably untrue, but Li Po more than likely would have agreed that it makes a great legend: During a boat party with friends, Li Po saw the reflection of the moon in the water. He drunkenly leaned out of the boat to give the "moon" a hug, fell into the water, and drowned.

Du Fu (712–770) was eleven years younger than Li Po but never would have been caught in such a foolish act. Du Fu wrote a lot about nature and even a few verses about wine. But the younger man never could be quite carefree. He was almost forty years old before his poetry attracted attention.

Du Fu took tragedy to heart. Just before the An Lu-shan rebellion, he wrote, "Inside the red gates, wine and meat go bad. On the roads are bones of men who died of cold." Many of his verses describe the suffering of ordinary people. Perhaps because of his compassion, the Chinese have traditionally admired Du Fu a little more than his jolly friend Li Po.

Loved for his compassion, Du Fu is admired for his almost awesome learning. Some of his poems contain so many literary and historical references that they cannot be translated.

reign of Emperor Xuan-cang. The older, Li Po, was known for his joy in life. The younger, Du Fu, wrote somewhat gloomier poems. The Chinese quote these two poets the way people in English-speaking countries quote the Bible or Shakespeare.

With the Stroke of a Brush . . .

Du Fu, Li Po, and all the other Tang poets didn't use pens to write their verses. They used brushes of animal hair with handles of bamboo. Their ink came dried in little blocks. To use it they rubbed the block on an inkstone, a flat rock with a little bowl in one end. They added water to the bowl and stirred the ink powder and water with the brush. Then they held these brushes straight up above the pages and wrote the characters without ever touching their hands or elbows to the paper. Try to write this way yourself. It's difficult!

It took years to master the basics of Chinese calligraphy. Children began to learn as soon as they started school. Many calligraphy styles had developed by Tang times. "Regular style" was standard, like block printing in English. In "running style" the characters looked like they were doing just that—running across the page. It compares to our cursive writing. "Grass style" was loose and more artistic; the calligrapher could express his feeling toward each word by the way he wrote it. Good students mastered all three styles and learned to make their characters "feel alive." The

SHENG: TO GIVE BIRTH

Over centuries, Chinese characters evolved and changed. In the beginning, many characters were recognizable pictures like the young plant shown above. Gradually, they became more stylized, less like pictures and more like "symbols," or groups of lines that stand for something.

The five characters at the left show the development of the character *sheng* (shung), which means "to give birth." The earliest character (below the plant) clearly looks like a little sprout trying to shoot up toward the sunlight. From this image, the character developed the meanings "to give birth," "to be born," and "to grow." The second character also looks like a plant. But bit by bit, the character changed, as the third and fourth characters show. The fifth character is the one used during the Tang dynasty and is still used today. It doesn't look much like a plant at all, but its basic meaning traces back to that first picture of a sprout.

Chinese believed that you could judge a person's character and intelligence by his or her handwriting.

Very few examples of Tang books have survived. This fragment from a book was found in a Tang temple complex in far western China. It took years to learn to write the neat characters on these eighth-century C.E. pages. The top character in the far left column means "man."

Pictures Worth a Thousand Words

At the imperial court, Tang artists created beautiful portraits and pictures of religious scenes. Wu Tao-yuan (woo tao-you-ANN), also known as Wu Tao-zi (woo tao-zuh), was the most famous. He devoted his career to painting murals for temples and monasteries. Thousands of admirers used to gather to watch him paint the walls of these sacred places. His images looked so real, it was said, that horses galloped out of his paintings and birds flew out of his scenes. Another legend claims that he left this earth by disappearing into one of his own paintings. Unfortunately, war and time destroyed the buildings he decorated. Nothing of his work survives.

Some examples of a different sort of Tang painting, landscapes, do still exist. The idea of painting natural scenes, such as a river valley or a mountain range, first developed during the Tang. Some of the Tang landscape paintings were colorful and realistic. Many Chinese mountains really do shoot up into the sky like the

ones in artwork. Other landscapes were done only in black and white and left lots of open space. These paintings tried to capture a mood, like a poem does. In the centuries that followed, landscapes would become a dominant form of Chinese art. Some say landscapes are China's major artistic contribution to the world.

Tang "Pop Culture"

Every scholar had to learn poetry and calligraphy. Gradually during the Tang dynasty, scholars took up painting as well. In later dynasties, scholar-officials came to trace their tradition of painting back to the Tang. From a scholar-official's point of view, the only arts worth serious attention were poetry, calligraphy, and painting. But Chinese culture created far more than these.

During the Tang, stories gained great popularity. People talked about the latest tales the way we now talk about music videos. Many people made their living by telling fairy tales in the two big marketplaces in Chang-an, often acting out the stories. Many years later these acted-out stories would evolve into plays. Chinese folktales had many different topics; the more exotic, or strange and foreign, the better. Some Chinese stories seem similar to Western tales. In "The Bear's Husband" a giant can smell humans, just like the "fee-fi-fo-fum" giant in "Jack and the Beanstalk." The Chinese also tell a story similar to "Cinderella."

The grand people at the imperial court pretended to look down on these folktales, but that didn't stop them from copying them and retelling them in fancier language. Storytellers were some of the most popular entertainers at court.

During the Tang dynasty great accomplishments

Landscape painting first became a major art form during the Tang, and the style was copied until modern times. This example dates to 1580 C.E., during the Ming dynasty.

were also achieved in ceramics and sculpture. Artisans created ceramic figurines for decoration and also for burial in tombs. Tang figures of horses are very graceful and are still prized today. Earlier Chinese statues, like Egyptian statues, were stiff and not very realistic. Tang artists carved statues that were more rounded and a little more lifelike.

Of all the ceramic figures that survive from the Tang, the horses are the most prized. This sculpture of a woman on horseback is finished in a mixture of green, rust, and cream-colored glaze typical of Tang figurines.

Pilgrims still travel to see the huge Da-fu *carved out of a cliff in Sichuan Province. It takes about thirty minutes to climb from the statue's base to its head.*

Many statues were also enormous. A monk started sculpting the *Da-fu* (DAH-foo), or "Big Buddha," in Sichuan (suh-CHOO-ahn) during the reign of the first Tang emperor. It took ninety years to finish, and it's huge. The Buddha has been carved out of a cliff on a river and stands 156 feet (48 meters) high. The Buddha's ears are longer than a two-story house is high; you could have a picnic on the statue's big toenail!

The Tang Chinese also had many scientific triumphs. Hundreds of years before Europeans did, they discovered that a combination of charcoal, sulfur, and saltpeter would explode. The mixture, which we know as gunpowder, was used mostly for fireworks rather than for warfare. They invented the wheelbarrow, a perfect device for carrying things through narrow village lanes. They used carved woodblocks to print books and pictures five hundred years before Europeans discovered the printing press. At a time when Europeans still thought the stars were fixed in an immense crystal, the Chinese had developed sophisticated astronomy. Imperial rules required court astronomers to define the four directions—north, south, east, and west—by observing the stars and sun. The Chinese produced the longest continuous record of celestial events until the rise of modern Western astronomy. Some Chinese star books cover periods for which there are no other accurate records.

No wonder the Chinese are proud of their four thousand years of history.

In this nineteenth-century print, a worker makes firecrackers, a uniquely Chinese invention. During the Tang, the Chinese lit firecrackers for holidays and religious ceremonies. They still do today.

CHAPTER THREE

A WORLD FILLED WITH MAGIC

The religion of Buddhism was one of the greatest inspirations for Tang artists. In this bronze statue from the eighth or ninth century, the Buddha is backed by a halo that represents the brilliance of his teachings. His right hand is lifted in a gesture that means "fear not."

To a person living in Tang dynasty China, magic and marvels filled every single day. Dragons brought the rain in spring and made the leaves fall in autumn. Spirits, both good and bad, inhabited every nook and cranny of the world: rocks, trees, streams, mountains, even doorways and stoves. Uncounted symbols and signs affected these spirits; so knowing the lucky seasons, days, directions, places, colors, and names could mean the difference between triumph and disaster. Not only this, but a family's ancestors, who became gods when they died, had to be honored and worshiped. The gods of the state "religion"—Confucianism—had to be respected. This meant sacrifices to ancient kings, wise men, and to the emperor himself. The great philosophies—Daoism and Buddhism—each included dozens of gods, great and small.

The Tang Chinese saw gods everywhere. Gods were part of the world, not outside the world or above it. Tang people didn't pour out their feelings in prayer to one all-powerful god. Instead they appealed to a crowd of gods.

Many different traditions blended in China. Day to day it was difficult to see where one ended and the next began. Considering them this way would be hopelessly confusing, so we'll take each tradition one at a time. First we'll look at ancient beliefs, then the philosophies of Confucianism, Daoism, and Buddhism. All of these beliefs had developed by the Tang dynasty. All of them still influence China today.

Ancient Traditions

How the Universe Came to Be

Most religions start with a story about how the world was formed. At first the Chinese told many origin myths. But by the time of the Tang dynasty, most Chinese accepted the following version:

The dragon, which lived under the water and in the clouds, was the most honored of Chinese symbols. In this embroidery, a five-clawed imperial dragon plays in the clouds with a pearl or disk that was believed to represent thunder.

In the beginning there was nothing but chaos. Slowly this disorganized mess hardened into a stone. Then the stone cracked like a cosmic egg, and a dwarf named Pan Ku came into being. It was his job to make order out of disorder. For eighteen thousand years he worked with tools to carve and shape the blocks of rock that floated in space.

Then Pan Ku the dwarf started to grow. He grew several feet every day. Finally Pan Ku stood hundreds of thousands of feet high. Then he died. His head became the mountains. His breath turned into the mist, clouds, and winds. His voice boomed across the land as thunder. His left eye became the light of the sun, his right eye, the moon, and his beard, the stars. His four limbs and five extremities (hands, feet, and top of his head) changed into the four quarters of the globe and the five mountains. His veins and muscles became the rivers, his flesh became the soil. His skin and hair bloomed into plants and trees. His teeth and bones hardened into minerals. The marrow in his bones crystallized into pearls and precious gems. His sweat covered the earth as rain. The parasites that had lived in his body—the fleas, mites, and worms that were part of everyday life—were blown across all creation. They became the people of the earth.

In time there came one called the True Prince, Shang-di (shong-dee). He floated up through the thirty-three heavens that Pan Ku had built and became the supreme god. Shang-di was also called the "White Jade Ruler." He lived in a castle of pale green crystal looking down on the thirty-three heavens and the earth at his feet. He ruled the universe.

Kings of Legend

Next came the job of creating civilization. A series of fabled rulers gave people the tools they needed to live. First came the Three Sovereigns. Fu-xi (foo-shee), the Ox Tamer, taught people how to tame animals and live together in families. Shen-nung, the Divine Farmer, invented the plow and the hoe. He explained how to farm and organize markets. Huang-di (huh-WANG-dee) introduced wooden houses, silk cloth, boats, carts, the bow and arrow, ceramics, and writing.

Besides being one of the Three Sovereigns, Huang-di was the first of a sequence of kings who came to be known as the Five Emperors. Of these the Chinese most respect Yao and Shun. Yao (yow) devised a calendar and a central government. He chose Shun, a poor peasant, to follow him. Shun became a model ruler. But floods troubled the reigns of Yao and Shun. Finally Shun asked an official named Yu (you) to control the water. Yu succeeded in building channels and draining the water out to sea. He became Shun's successor. Together, Yao, Shun, and Yu became known as the Three Sages, or wise men. The time that they ruled was called the Xia (SEE-ah) dynasty. The Shang and Zhou dynasties followed. Later the Chinese grouped them together as the Three Dynasties.

Throughout most of Chinese history, people accepted the Three Sovereigns, the Five Emperors, the Three Sages, and the Three Dynasties as fact. Generation after generation of Chinese students memorized the noble things these legendary rulers supposedly did. They were honored by national tradition, as George Washington is in the United States.

Gods and Symbols Everywhere

Many, many other ancient gods competed for the attention of the Tang Chinese. Not all of them had a wide national following. Every family had spirits only *they* worshiped, like those that inhabited their doorway or the courtyard. Other deities might lay claim to a village, a province, or a profession. Each god had a specific region or group of people that it protected.

People called upon these lesser gods for protection against this or that—for luck in business, for many sons, for a happy marriage. A person walking around Chang-an, or anywhere else in the Tang empire, would pass countless shrines and sanctuaries to this crowd of supernatural powers.

Symbols were also everywhere. They weren't gods, but they carried meaning and wishes, just as in the West today roses mean love and four-leaf clovers mean good luck. The Chinese painted symbols on their pottery, embroidered them into their clothes, carved them into their houses, drew them on paper, and pasted them on walls during holidays.

The king and queen of these special signs were the dragon and the phoenix. Unlike Western dragons that breathed fire, Chinese

Though it first appeared in the bronze art of the ancient Shang dynasty, a monster mask called a tao-tie *had become a standard symbol by Tang times. In this cup from the Tang dynasty, the handle comes out of the monster's mouth. The* tao-tie *is part dragon and part cow. It was supposed to warn against the dangers of greed.*

dragons ruled water. Rising to the clouds, they brought rain. Rising in rivers, they caused floods. When they surfaced on the sea, the tides came in. When they drank, the tides went out. In the springtime, they went up in the skies and fought one another. Rain and thunder resulted. In the autumn, they descended into the seas. They

Large pink peaches symbolize immortality and frequently appear in Chinese art. In this painting from the thirteenth century C.E., two figures offer a plate piled with "immortality peaches."

stayed there all winter (a cold, dry season in most of China) in gorgeous palaces beneath the waves. These magical creatures represented excellence and were the symbol of the emperor.

The dragon's partner was a mystical bird, the feng-huang (fung-HOO-anhg), loosely translated as "phoenix." It represented the sun and first appeared to announce the coming of the good kings: the Three Sovereigns and the Five Emperors. The phoenix only came to earth where there was something precious or when peace was there. Chinese empresses took the bird as their symbol. For this reason it often is shown paired with the dragon. This happened so frequently that engagement certificates came to be known as "dragon-phoenix papers," and wedding cakes were called "dragon-phoenix cakes."

Most other symbols expressed a wish for the Five Happinesses. Above all, the Chinese wished to (1) live long, (2) have great wealth, (3) be tranquil, (4) be virtuous, and (5) not die until achieving their destiny. Many things represented the wish for long life: tortoises, cranes, peaches, and knife-shaped mushrooms that never rot. Butterflies also stood for longevity because the Chinese word for butterfly, *tie* (TEE-eh), sounds like the word meaning "seventy or eighty." Flowers like peonies meant luxury. The color red stood for joy.

Chinese artists created dragons in every medium imaginable: painting, embroidery, sculpture, pottery, and jewelry. This golden dragon seems to be clawing at an invisible opponent.

How the World Worked

All these symbols, minor gods, and heroic kings existed in a world that the Tang Chinese believed was governed by very definite rules. They thought that everything in creation was divided between two forces: Yin and Yang (yong). The character for Yin was originally a picture of hills and shadows. Yin is associated with clouds and rain, with the idea of femaleness, winter, and the inside. Yang, in contrast, was represented by a character of slanting sun rays. Yang was connected with sunshine and warmth, maleness, summer, and the outside. Both Yin and Yang were present in everything; sometimes the Yin dominated and sometimes the Yang did.

The two forces of Yin and Yang combined with the forces of the Five Elements to control the cycles of the universe. The Five

Elements were the five fundamental sorts of matter or fundamental processes: earth, wood, metal, fire, and water. Each followed another that it could not conquer—that is, earth is inferior to wood because in the form of a shovel wood can dig it up; wood is defeated by metal, which cuts it; metal loses to fire, which melts it; fire, in turn, is vanquished by water, which puts it out. Finally the circle is closed when water is tamed by earth, which channels and dams it.

Rules governing the Two Forces and the Five Elements were brought together in an ancient book called the *I Ching* (ee ching). The *I Ching* started out as a collection of methods for telling the future. It developed into a dizzying, complicated system of symbols and their explanations. The book was founded on sixty-four combinations of six lines that are either broken or unbroken. The broken lines stood for *Yin*, the female, or soft. The unbroken lines stood for *Yang,* the male, or hard. The combinations of six lines were called hexagrams.

The Chinese believed that the way these hexagrams related to the Five Elements could explain anything that happened in the universe. The Chinese wrote volumes about this basic system. The ideas in the *I Ching* gave rise to all sorts of fortune-telling methods: magic numbers, the study of faces to tell the future, the study of the landscape. All related back to Yin, Yang, and the Five Elements. Everything took part in an endless seesawing back and forth between Yin and Yang. It was a complicated world indeed!

What Confucius Said

In Tang China nothing affected day-to-day life more than the teachings of a man called Confucius. Actually his name was Kung Qiu (kong CHEE-o). The Chinese gave him the respectful title of Grand Master Kung, or Kung Fu-zi (kong FOO-zuh). When Westerners tried to repeat that name the best they could come up with was *Confucius.*

Confucius was born in 551 B.C.E. He grew up in the small kingdom of Lu (lou) in what is now northeastern China. His family was noble, but his father died when Confucius was only three years old. So Confucius never had very much money.

Confucius grew up to become China's first professional

teacher. Students paid him to teach them his views on life and government. Many of these scholars quickly rose to high positions in the government. Confucius, however, never held more than a minor government post, such as a tax collector or a cattle keeper. When he was middle-aged, he spent ten years traveling to the various small kingdoms that made up China. He was trying to convince one of the rulers to put his ideas into practice. But during Confucius's life, no ruler ever did.

The man who rose to be the most revered thinker in all of China was a very human man. The fact that he never got appointed to a high post made him cranky. He complained that he never got the right sort of students. He could be rude. Despite all this Confucius

Scholars and their children study a drawing of Yin and Yang on a length of silk. In the circle, the black half is Yin and the white half is Yang. Notice that the Yin side has a dot of white, or Yang. The Yang side has a dot of black, or Yin. This expresses the idea that opposites complement each other.

liked to tease his students, and he appreciated a good joke.

The reason this far-from-saintly person became beloved by the Chinese was that he had an unshakable faith in human goodness. Confucius lived during a period of discord, when China was divided into a dozen or more small kingdoms constantly battling one another. Barbarians to the north and west pressed in on China. Confucius rose above this confusion. He insisted that men could live on a higher plane than animals, without fighting and injustice. He said that people should try to be good, not because they fear punishment, but because it's the right thing to do.

Confucius didn't spend much time thinking about life after death. Instead he was concerned with the here and now, with how people could live together peacefully. He claimed that he was merely repeating ideas from the golden age of the Three Sovereigns, the Five Emperors, and all those legendary rulers. In fact Confucius's ideas *were* new to the Chinese. Their very early history is a story of "might makes right." If you had the stronger warriors and the bigger army, what you said was law. Confucius suggested that power should come from a completely different source—virtue.

This image of Confucius comes from a rubbing of a relief from the Ming dynasty. In it, the philosopher seems to be laughing. Despite his serious ideas, he is said to have enjoyed humor.

Before Confucius the titles for China's leaders translate roughly as "warrior-official" and "son of a ruler." Confucius transformed these into titles meaning "men who do the right thing." The highest power, Confucius said, was something called *ren* (run), which means "goodness," or, "a sensitive concern for other people." A man of virtue shows his goodness and concern through *li* (lee), or "proper conduct." As one of Confucius's most famous sayings notes, "A leader is like the wind. The common people are like grass. When the wind blows, the grass always bends."

Based on *ren* and *li,* Confucius's prescription for living went something like this: What is the greatest good? It is the good of the state. How is this attained? By good government. What is it that gives some men the power to rule over others? Virtue, or right behavior. How does a man achieve this virtue? By knowing himself and

Anyone who has ever been to a Chinese restaurant and opened a fortune cookie has probably read something like, "Confucius says ..." That phrase is usually followed with some bewildering statement like, "A melon on the top of a roof may roll either of two ways."

Did Confucius really say those things? Probably not. But it's easy to get the impression that China's foremost philosopher did have a fortune-cookie way of thinking. This is because the only written record of the sage's views on life are collected in a book called the *Lun-yu* (LOON-you). The title means "Conversations," but is usually translated as "Analects." The *Lun-yu* can be pretty confusing to read. It is mostly a collection of sentences that start, "The Master said ..." Most of the statements don't have any context. That is, nothing tells the reader why or when Confucius said the things he did or what he was talking about. Here are a few of the most quoted of Confucius's words that really were said by the sage:

It is only the wisest and the stupidest who cannot change.
Silence is a friend who will never betray.
Don't do unto others what you yourself would not like.
In education there are no class distinctions.
The way of the gentleman is threefold: Being humane, he has no anxieties;
    being wise, he has no doubts; being brave, he has no fear.
Judge others by what you know of yourself. That is the way to humanity.
A father should shield a son; a son should shield a father.
Love men.

Next time you open a fortune cookie, enjoy the riddle, but don't assume Confucius was its author.

human nature. How does a man acquire this knowledge? By studying ancient literature—the deeds of the Three Sovereigns and the Five Emperors.

Since no ruler during Confucius's time was willing to put this advice into practice, Confucius and his ideas could have been lost to history. They were not lost because in the following centuries several brilliant men championed the notions set forth by Confucius. By Tang times Confucianism was the dominant set of beliefs in society. Knowledge of his philosophy was necessary to do just about anything.

Followers of Confucius focused on Five Key Relationships. In order of importance these were father-son, ruler-subject, brother-brother, husband-wife, and friend-friend. Notice that the tie between father and son comes before that between ruler and subject. The tie between husband and wife is pretty low on the scale, number four.

In all these relationships, people were supposed to cultivate Five Virtues—(1) father and son should cultivate "filial piety": the son should obey the father, the father should look out for the son; (2) ruler and subjects should be loyal to one another; (3) brothers should be "brotherly," or kind and supportive; (4) husbands and wives should work at love and obedience: the husbands loving and the wives obeying; and (5) friends should be faithful to one another. All this meant a reverence for superiors and kindness and fairness to equals and subordinates.

Confucianism didn't tell people what to do if one relationship or one virtue conflicted with another. For instance what should a son do if his father was not filial? Should a subject follow the orders of a ruler who was unwise? Confucian teaching didn't give any concrete answers to these questions. Confucian thought advised: Think about it! Worry about it! If you have cultivated virtue in yourself, you'll be able to figure things out.

Following "the Way"

At about the same time Confucius was trying to persuade rulers to put his ideas into action, another way of thinking was developing. The wars and conflict of the time led Confucius to focus on society, on people and their relationships to one another. Other thinkers went in the opposite direction—they decided to turn away from the human world. These rebels wanted to ignore society's rules, go off into the woods, and learn to live in harmony with nature. They were not interested in cultivating relationships or arguing about virtues; they cared about balance. They called themselves Daoists.

These thinkers were inspired by the vision of an all-embracing, cosmic process called the *Dao* (dow). The character for Dao is made up of a head and the sign for "going." In many ways it is untranslatable. Dao means many things: the way, the order of nature, the power behind things. The Dao is sort of the what, the how, and the why of everything. The other important thing to the Daoists was the concept of *qi* (chee). This character is made up of the picture of "breath." It sort of means "soul," or the "essence" of being. People tried to find their *qi*, or soul, by following the Dao, or Way. (They also cultivated their *qi* to find the Dao.)

If this sounds like a confusing riddle, that's because it is. To the Daoists the world *was* a riddle. That was okay. Finding the right answer wasn't as important to them as just asking questions and observing. In some ways the Daoists were sort of early environmentalists. They didn't believe in doing anything against the Way, or Dao, of nature. They used the old ideas of Yin and Yang to promote an idea of balance between hard and soft, light and dark, aggressive and passive, and so on. Peace came from accepting that things were always shifting back and forth between Yin and Yang, that things would always change.

Perhaps it's fitting that Lao-zi (lao-zuh), the founder of this mystical philosophy, should be one of the most shadowy figures in Chinese history. Some Chinese believe that he was an ancient god or an ancient emperor. Some say he was a royal librarian and that he lived to the ripe old age of 160 years.

Though no one is quite sure who Lao-zi was, the "father of Daoism" inspired many artists. This fresco, or wall painting, calls Lao-zi the "Lord of the Southern Dipper."

41

Whatever the facts of his life, it is probable that Lao-zi wrote the book that became the bible for the Daoists. Sometimes it is called the *Lao-zi,* after its author. Sometimes it is called the *Dao De Jing* (dow duh JING), meaning "The Classic of the Way and of Virtue." Many have judged this the most beautiful and profound book ever written in Chinese. It is a short work, only five thousand words, most of it poetry. It is full of puzzling statements, such as "The man who withdraws from the world, finds it"; or "By giving up power, he becomes powerful"; and "By not desiring riches, he becomes rich."

Another philosopher, Chuang-zi (choo-ANG-zuh), produced the second great text of Daoism. If the *Lao-zi* was a puzzle, the *Chuang-zi* was even more fantastic. In it, animals and insects debate philosophy and men float about in the air. With this text Daoism turned its back on politics completely, saying, "The wise man knows it is better to be alone with the Dao than to be the ruler of the whole world."

At first Daoism was a philosophy of solitary wise men, quietly meditating in forests and on mountaintops. Gradually the Daoists developed ideas that made their philosophy popular with ordinary people. The Daoists came to believe that by following the magic processes of the Dao, they could ride on the winds and live forever. This led some to try bizarre chemistry experiments, breathing exercises, gymnastics, and other efforts to escape death. The idea of immortality spread to the common people. Gradually Daoism developed into an organized religion of sorts. It grew to have monasteries, temples, saints, and sacred texts. It borrowed a few of the old nature gods, continued the ideas of Yin and Yang, and came up with some gods of its own.

The desire never to die led the Daoists to create a sacred group of Eight Immortals and still another paradise for them. The tradition wasn't fully developed until the end of the Tang dynasty, but it became central to popular belief. This paradise lay to the east, off the coast of China.

How a Prince Named Siddhartha Became Buddha

The last of the three great religions of China is Buddhism. The teachings of Buddha filtered into China from India about the time

of Christ, but they were slow to catch on. During the Tang dynasty Chinese Buddhism became more powerful than it had ever been. Buddhism inspired a large part of the painting and sculpture of the Tang. Monasteries dedicated to Buddha became centers of learning. The common people looked forward to the many festivals held at Buddhist temples. As the Tang dynasty neared its end, Buddhism had become tremendously powerful. As a result late Tang emperors persecuted the monks in Buddhist temples. Buddhism in China never again regained the power it had had during the Tang dynasty, but it continued to influence Chinese thought.

Buddhism is based on the teachings of a man who lived around 500 B.C.E., in what is now the southern edge of Nepal, north of India. His birth was said to be a miracle. Rather than being born the usual way, he sprang from his mother's side as she rested beneath a grove of trees. His mother belonged to a noble family named Sakya (sock-EE-ah). She named him Prince Siddhartha (sid-HEARTH-ah). The legends say that Siddhartha grew up sheltered from all the pains of the world. He lived in a beautiful marble palace filled with silk

Two Buddhist "guardian" gods keep watch over a temple complex at Luoyang in central China. During most of the Tang dynasty, sculptors busily shaped figures like these out of the cliff walls and caves on the banks of the Yi River. Before the end of the dynasty, they had completed more than 100,000 such images and statues. Many of the caves and cliffs were protected by temples built around them. The square holes in between the two large figures once held beams that supported the temples. After the persecution of Buddhists in the late-Tang period, the art of Buddhist cave sculpture died in China.

hangings and soft rugs. He ate delicious food. So that he would never be bored, Siddhartha's parents put on all sorts of entertainments such as concerts and circuses. So that he would never want to leave home they surrounded their prince with beautiful young girls.

Despite all these efforts to shelter him, Siddhartha started to wonder about what lay outside the walls of his family's palace. When he became a young man, he decided to find out. On four separate nights he sneaked past the palace walls to see the world beyond. What he found upset him.

The Four Encounters

The first night, the prince met an old man leaning on a staff. He asked the man why he looked so weak and tired. "Haven't you ever seen old age?" the elderly man asked. The prince hadn't. He returned to the palace very puzzled.

The second night, Siddhartha passed a house where a man lay propped up in bed. The man shivered and moaned. The prince asked him why he was acting like that. "Haven't you ever seen sickness before?" the man asked. Siddhartha hadn't. That night he went home worried.

The third night, the prince again crept out of the palace. Soon he passed a man lying very still and completely wrapped in cloth. The prince turned to a person and asked why the man was lying there like that. "What?" the passerby said. "Do you mean to tell me you've never seen a dead person before?" But Siddhartha hadn't. He returned to his comfortable palace, very confused indeed.

The fourth night, Siddhartha went out into the world and met a man in rags. The man was very skinny and had shaved off all of his hair. He held out an empty bowl to the prince and looked at him, pleading with his eyes. "What do you want?" the prince asked. "Why are you wearing such tattered clothes?" The begging man looked surprised and said, "Haven't you ever seen poverty before?" But the prince had not. He returned to his luxurious home very upset.

Seeing the outside world had made Siddhartha wonder: How could his wonderful life in the palace exist in a world where there was also old age, sickness, death, and poverty? The prince decided he could not continue the way he had been living. He decided to leave his family and his palace.

One night he rode away from the palace on his horse Kanthaka. He rode out of the city gates and far away. Siddhartha spent his days thinking about life and suffering and what it all meant. Finally, while sitting under a *bodhi* tree, a sort of fig tree, the answers came to him in a blinding flash. He became "enlightened." He became Buddha.

Eternal Bliss

At the time Siddhartha turned into a Buddha, most Indians believed that people lived, died, and were reborn endlessly. Whether you were reborn as a person or as an insect depended on your good and bad deeds, your karma. The final goal was to stop this cycle of birth, death, and rebirth. Doing so was called nirvana, a word that literally means "a snuffing out," like a candle with no more wick to burn. Nirvana also came to mean "eternal bliss." Buddha built on these old ideas but came up with a radically different solution to the never-ending cycle.

Buddha said that the world is an illusion. He claimed there was no "report card" of good and bad deeds, no karma. What keeps people in this unreal world is their attachment to life. If a person wants to stop the merry-go-round of life—suffering, death, and rebirth—the person has to realize that he is on the merry-go-round because he wants to be. Getting off the merry-go-round and reaching nirvana isn't difficult, it's simple. All a person has to do is to let go.

This Tang painting on silk shows Buddha's Four Encounters. From top to bottom: *Young Prince Siddhartha confronts first old age, then sickness, death, and finally, poverty.*

THE PILGRIMAGE OF THE MONK XUAN-CANG

At its height Buddhism exerted a powerful pull on the Chinese people—so much so that many felt they had to go to India to get accurate scriptures based on the Buddha's teachings. From a modern perspective, that doesn't sound like such a big deal. After all, today you could probably find Buddhist scriptures on the Internet. If you really wanted to, you could get on a plane and go to India to learn about Buddhism. But in the seventh and eighth centuries, things weren't that simple . . . not by a long shot.

In those days most books were copied by hand. Someone might have a Buddhist scripture when he went to visit a friend. The friend copied it, changed it a little, perhaps shortening a sentence here and there. Then the friend went to visit another friend. That friend copied it again, changing it a little more. This process happened over and over, like a long, drawn-out version of the playground game telephone. As in that game, the version that made its way to the Chinese capital of Chang-an may have been completely different from the original that started out in India.

If a Chinese person wanted to go to the source, to get the *real* scriptures, he would have to attempt a terrifying journey. He would have to walk for weeks, months, and years through the deserts and wild lands of western China and then turn south, climbing over some of the highest mountains in the world, the Himalayas. To bring the sacred books back, he would have to retrace all those difficult steps. At least two hundred people are known to have made the trip.

The most famous of these scripture-seekers was a Chinese monk named Xuan-cang. He set out from the Tang capital of Chang-an in 629. He traveled from the capital to the city of Lan-zhou (lawn-joe), which lies nestled among dry, rolling hills. Then the monk started to follow the Silk Road, the track that Arab traders used to bring Chinese goods to the West. He walked more than 1,500 miles (2,414 kilometers) along this famous trade route. Then he turned south, climbed the Himalayas, and entered India. He traveled to the birthplace of Buddhism and spent years debating religious scholars and collecting Buddhist texts.

Xuan-cang returned to the Tang capital in 645, after sixteen long years away from home. He brought with him six hundred original texts of Buddhist writings. The emperor was so impressed that he gave the monk a salary for life and built a tall tower, the "big-goose pagoda," to house all the scriptures. The pagoda still stands, and legends of the achievements of Xuan-cang are still told today.

Buddha came up with a twelve-step plan to help people reach eternal bliss. First, a person had to accept the Four Noble Truths: (1) suffering exists; (2) desire causes suffering; (3) suffering can end; and (4) suffering ends when desire ends. In everyday terms this means that if you're miserable because you want a boy or girl to like you, or if you want your parents to buy you a new video game, the solution is to stop wanting those things in the first place. Of course this is much easier to say than to do. So, to help people learn to stop wanting things, Buddha had a method called the Eightfold Path. It required believers to leave society, live in monasteries, and focus on achieving nirvana. Everyone who reached nirvana became a Buddha, too.

Just as there are many kinds of Christians—Catholics, Lutherans, Methodists, Baptists—there grew to be many kinds of Buddhists. Mainly, however, there are two groups. The first is the original kind of Buddhism—only the few that agree to reject the world can be saved. The second kind of Buddhism expands the circle—everyone can be saved if only they have enough faith. The Chinese favored the second kind of Buddhism. The sects that grew to power in China stressed salvation for all. Being saved required being devoted to various saints and Buddhas.

Most Chinese Buddhist temples had shrines to many bodhisattvas (boh-dih-SUHT-vuhz). These sacred beings were like Western saints. They had achieved enough enlightenment to enter nirvana and become Buddhas. Instead they decided to help others along the Eightfold Path to nirvana. Wearing crowns and robes of jewels, bodhisattvas ruled over paradises that were like rest stops on the way to full Buddhahood. Winning the favor of one of these saints, the Chinese believed, was the passport to enter one of these paradises. That way, they would gain temporary protection from the painful cycle of birth and death. For most believers this became the ultimate religious goal. Nirvana, the "snuffing out," became a remote ideal.

The "big-goose pagoda" (left) was originally built in 652 C.E. to house scriptures that the Buddhist monk Xuan-cang brought back from India. The pagoda was rebuilt during the last imperial dynasty and is open to visitors.

CHAPTER FOUR

A TAPESTRY OF LEGEND AND LIFE

Chinese beliefs came alive in their art, their clothes, their buildings, even in their hair ornaments and decorations. This plaque might have been hung on a wall. It represents a mythical animal with long horns, one of dozens upon dozens of magical animals the Chinese created. A Tang dynasty artisan hammered this beautiful image out of silver.

The average person living in Chang-an probably didn't think much about the whys and wherefores of the gods. Suppose someone had asked, "Why are you lighting a stick of incense in that temple?" A Chinese person of Tang times would no doubt have answered, "That's just the way things are. Why do you ask?" It would be the same as if someone asked why you shake hands with someone new.

It's challenging to understand what people believe. It is even more challenging to understand why people believe what they do and how their beliefs affect the way they act. Learning how beliefs affected day-to-day life under the Tang paints a picture of what it might have been like to live in China thirteen hundred years ago. It is also interesting to examine how day-to-day life may have shaped the kind of beliefs the Chinese came to hold. Once again, we'll look at the major belief systems one by one.

Confucian Ideals at Home and Work

By the Tang dynasty most of Chinese society had incorporated the ideas of Confucius—the importance of virtue, loyalty, and rules of behavior. Children understood these concepts when they were barely old enough to talk. That's because Confucian philosophy had a huge influence on two major parts of life: the family and the workplace. A person couldn't talk to an elder, eat a meal, ask a boss for advice, or do anything else without paying attention to the many rules that grew out of Confucian thought.

The Tang Chinese considered filial piety, or respect for elders and superiors, a great virtue. In this painting from the twelfth century C.E., a man shows respect for an elder by doing a ke-tou, *kneeling and touching his head to the ground.*

It all began with the family. During the Tang dynasty a particular sort of Confucian family became the ideal. It became the foundation of most Chinese ideas of right and wrong, and largely remains so to this day. Not everyone lived this way. But a Chinese subject of the Tang would consider you lucky if you had the kind of life described below:

You live in a large house with several generations of relatives—grandparents, parents, uncles, aunts, cousins, brothers, sisters. The "house" is really a collection of houses surrounded by a high brick

49

In this portrait, clothes show rank. The founder of the Tang dynasty is wearing clothes only an emperor could wear: a robe of yellow, the imperial color, decorated with a five-clawed dragon.

wall. It is laid out sort of like a school campus. Important meetings and family meals take place in a large main hall. You and your family members spend most of your time in clusters of rooms around one of a series of courtyards. You live in a section with your parents and siblings. Your cousins live with their parents—your aunts and uncles—in a different section. Your father's parents have a set of rooms.

Where your room is, how big it is, where you sit at the dinner table, how nice your clothes are, and a million other small details depend on where you fit in the family hierarchy. In other words, everyone has a rank. The oldest male, the grandfather, stands at the top of the heap, the youngest female servant at the bottom. As a child, your rank is somewhere in the middle. Older and male is always better.

Confucius stressed that juniors must honor their superiors, so if you are the first son of a first son, you can boss your siblings and cousins around. At meals you are served before any of the other kids, but you start eating only after your elders pick up their chopsticks. You owe absolute obedience to your seniors—your father, mother, and older relatives. You don't even think about disobeying your parents or talking back to them. When you go to pay respects to your grandfather you kneel in front of him and touch your head to the floor several times. This is called doing a *ke-tou* (KUH-tow), sometimes translated as "kow-tow." After your grandfather dismisses you, you shuffle out of the room backward. It is extremely rude to turn your back on a superior.

If your family is very lucky, your father or one of your other male relatives passed the difficult examinations and has become an imperial official. At work, this relative observes a whole other set of rankings and regulations. Each rank has a special color, and there are rules about what hats and belts can be worn, even the number of courses that officials of a certain rank can serve at a feast.

CHINA'S EXAMINATION NIGHTMARE

If you get nervous thinking about next week's history test, be glad that you don't have to take the exams the Chinese took during the Tang dynasty and continued to take until the early twentieth century. They were worse than finals, worse than the Scholastic Achievement Tests (SATs). They were more difficult than just about anything the modern world has to offer. But if you wanted to become an official—which was the best way to money and power in imperial China—you had to pass the tests.

A young Chinese boy started learning to memorize and take exams from the minute he began his schooling at the age of six or seven. All together that meant committing to memory a total of more than 400,000 words. If he was smart and worked hard, he might be ready for the imperial exams by the time he was in his late twenties or early thirties.

In order to reach the highest level, he had to spend years taking a series of exams—one at the local level, one at the provincial level, and another at the national level. The whole course of a man's life could be determined by how he coped with the following ordeal:

By law, the provincial-level tests were held every three years, in September. The emperor dispatched imperial examiners to all the provincial capitals. Each capital had a permanent group of buildings, a compound, where examinations were conducted. These were huge, barnlike buildings, a honeycomb of thousands of little rooms, each just large enough to hold one man. The rooms had no doors and no furniture.

At dawn on the day of the exam thousands of men lined up at the front gate of the test compound. They had to bring their own food, bedding, writing materials, and a curtain to hang across the doorway to their room. At the front gate soldiers inspected their belongings. No books or papers with any kind of writing were allowed.

Then the scholars trudged into the compound with their luggage and their hopes. Once all were in, the gates were sealed. Neither the candidates nor the officials judging them could leave. If someone had the misfortune to die while the test was still in progress, the officials had no choice but to wrap the deceased in straw matting and throw the body over the wall.

The test consisted of three sets of essay questions. Students could write out rough drafts of their answers, but once they started working in their official answer books, they could not make any corrections or cross out any characters. It took almost a week to finish.

The pressure was intense. After studying for years it all came down to the student and his answer book, alone in an uncomfortable room, perhaps wet and cold, away from the support of teachers and family. One mistaken character, one slip of the brush, and the answer would be disqualified. He would have to wait another three years to try again. Under such harsh conditions it was common for men to get sick or even to go insane.

After answering all the questions the dazed candidates staggered out of the compound. Then the wait began. It took almost a month for the officials to grade the answers. For those who had passed, the world changed overnight. The day before, they had been unimportant, penniless students. Now they were men of substance. If they passed the final test in the national capital, the world lay at their feet.

These rules go down to minute details like this: Only the emperor can wear robes decorated with five-clawed dragons; princes can wear four-clawed dragons; very high officials may be allowed to wear dragons with three claws.

Confucius taught that virtue was what gave some men the right to rule over others. By the time of the Tang dynasty, this had come to mean the ability to observe *li,* or proper behavior, in this complex hierarchy of ranks and rules. You spend most of your education learning to do this. It affects even the smallest things you do, such as how you address your relatives. For instance it really matters if your cousin is the child of a second-born son or of a firstborn son. So there are separate words for "daughter of the second uncle" and "daughter of the first uncle." It also matters if the uncle is from your mother's side of the family or your father's side. Taking into account age, birth order, and the side of the family, you have to learn more than two dozen names for relatives.

Ranks also affected the law, or the Tang Code. For instance, if you lift a hand against your parents or grandparents, you can be beheaded. If you hit an older brother or sister, you might be sentenced to two-and-a-half years of hard labor. But if you hit an older cousin, you might only get one hundred strokes of the rod. Nothing is absolutely wrong or absolutely right. It depends on relationships.

So, as you make your way in your family and in society, you do everything you can to bind yourself to someone more powerful. You have few, if any, relationships with equals. You deal either with superiors or inferiors.

Old Beliefs Become Confucian

Chinese society had already been around a long time when Confucius came up with his philosophy. As the Chinese incorporated Confucian ideas into every part of their lives, they were unwilling to give up many old traditions. The solution? They just started describing old beliefs and practices in Confucian terms.

One of the oldest Chinese ideas was the belief that the emperor was above ordinary men and negotiated with the gods so that they would bring rain and plentiful harvests. After Confucius, the emperors continued to make annual sacrifices to the gods at the

IF YOU LIVED IN TANG CHINA

If you had been born in China during the time of the Tang rulers, your way of life would have been determined by the facts of your birth—whether you were a girl or a boy, whether you were wealthy or poor. With this chart you can trace the course your life might have taken as a member of an upper-class family during the rule of the Tang dynasty.

You were born in Chang-an. . . .

As a Boy . . .

As a Girl . . .

You live with your parents, grandparents, aunts, uncles, cousins, and siblings in a one-story house of wood and brick with a tile roof. The house is built around one, or several courtyards, and includes a large garden.

Until age 7 you play in your family's courtyards while your nurse watches. You play with kites, pinwheels, and balls. You learn to play Chinese chess and to write simple poems.

▼

At age 7 you go to school full time, or your family hires a tutor to teach you at home. At first you learn twenty new characters a day. Later you have to learn one hundred or more new characters each day. You study the *Four Books and the Five Classics* and prepare for the imperial exams. Your parents put a lot of pressure on you to do well.

▼

At age 20 at the Festival of the Dead in April, you receive a ceremonial cap and become an adult. If you thought early school was hard, now you begin intense studying for the imperial exams. If you don't do well in the exams, you help with the family business.

▼

Soon you marry, but still live at your parents' house with your new family. If you have enough money, you may add concubines to your family. These women are not your wives, but your children by them are considered legitimate. Perhaps after many years of work and study, you may become an imperial official. You retire at age 68.

Until age 7 you play games with your brothers, sisters, and cousins. Sometimes, you may even visit the sweet sellers and toy sellers in the streets.

▼

At age 7 you learn sewing, weaving, embroidery, and a little bit of poetry and literature. If you live toward the end of the dynasty, you have your feet wrapped tightly with strips of cloth. After years of being bound, your feet will be folded under and be half of their normal size. This is called a "lotus foot."

▼

At age 15 in April, you come of age. Hairpins are placed in your hair at the Festival of the Dead. Then your family begins looking for a husband for you. The man you marry will be older, but probably only by a few years. You don't meet your husband until your wedding day. After this, you see your original family only rarely.

▼

As a young wife, your main goal is to be modest, faithful to your husband, and to produce a son. After you become a mother, your status in your new family is secure. If your husband dies, his wealth goes to your sons, who must care for you until you die.

When you die, your family holds a lavish funeral. Back in the old house, both men and women ascend to the sacred status of "ancestor" and an altar to them is placed in the main room.

Almost all Chinese families had altars dedicated to their ancestors where they made offers of fruit, flowers, and incense. Similar offerings have been made before this altar dedicated to Confucius.

Temple of Heaven and the Temple of Earth, and so on. These gods didn't have much to do with Confucius, but the emperor started to honor the gods in a Confucian way. The emperor became the fatherly leader, or patriarch, of the nation. He made sacrifices to nature gods who were assigned ranks just like officials.

Likewise, when Confucius started teaching, the Chinese had already been worshiping their dead ancestors for as long as anyone could remember. So they just added ancestor worship to the whole Confucian philosophy. When a near relation died, each member of the family would go into deep mourning. How much a person mourned depended on how close the relative had been.

After death, an ancestor continued to play a role in the Confucian world of the living. Near an altar in the main room of the house, a stone tablet, engraved with the name of the dead ancestor, would be set up. Descendants always remembered to honor these tablets. They regularly set offerings of food before them. Honoring dead ancestors, once an ancient pagan practice, became the most civilized, Confucian thing a Chinese person could do.

Daoist Free Spirits

Throughout the last two thousand years there have always been people who thought following the Dao, the Way, meant going off into the forest or up to the mountains to be a hermit in tune with nature. But for the rest of the Chinese, living in the workaday Confucian world, Daoist ideas still had an impact.

Whether in a forest or in the busy streets of Chang-an, following the Dao meant to "go along and get along." Daoists believed that they gained power by giving up power. So it became popular wisdom that the wise and powerful man was the one who gave in, who let others have their way, who yielded instead of fought. Following the Dao involved observing this natural way of yielding. It meant not doing anything against the natural order.

Daoists also believed in *qi,* what might be called the "essence of life." It was somewhat like "the Force" that Luke Skywalker finds in the *Star Wars* movies. Taking care of one's *qi,* and thus following the Dao, could lead to better health and a longer life. Some Daoists limited themselves to diets of what can only be described as health food—vegetables and low-fat grains.

The Daoists also developed gymnastic routines that were supposed to keep the body in line with the Dao. Early in the morning in Chang-an many people would be up at dawn going through very slow motions that imitated the movements of certain animals. These routines were supposed to make the *qi* circulate along certain channels. The Daoists called this *qi gong* (CHEE gohng), which translates as "working your *qi.*" This discipline was supposed to bring peace and health to those who practiced it. Gradually *qi gong* developed into many different styles, some with fantastic names like praying-mantis style. Some of these variations were very athletic, even violent. They evolved into the martial arts now called kung fu.

The observation of nature inspired by the Daoists also contributed to the development of Chinese medicine. Traditional Chinese doctors relied on catalogs of herbs and their effects. Doctors collected this knowledge in huge illustrated books the size of encyclopedias. *The Treasury of the Way* includes almost six thousand volumes on subjects ranging from herbal medicine to chemistry to physical education. Some of the wisdom included: Cooked leeks improve the appetite; yams put people to sleep; dried apricots help heart disease; licorice is good for just about anything. Some of the recipes in these books could be incredibly complicated to make. One cure might call for twenty-five ingredients—everything from ground buffalo horn and dried spiders to aged orange peels.

During the Tang dynasty much of medical theory concerned how these herbal cures interacted with a patient's *qi*. The Daoist idea of *qi* was closely linked to the idea of channels. They believed vital energy circulated along main paths and crosspaths, much like roads in a city or veins in the body. By inserting a needle at a certain point in the body, Chinese doctors believed they could link sensitive points. The holes made by the needles would also provide an escape route for evil spirits imprisoned in the tissue. This would cure pain and disease as well, the theory went. In the West we call this method acupuncture. Modern scientists believe that it somehow works on the nervous system. In modern times some Chinese patients have undergone serious surgery without anesthesia by having acupuncture instead. Many patients, suffering from arthritis or muscle pain, who do not find help from Western medicine, also turn to acupuncture.

Cheating Death

As we've seen, influence was a two-way street. Tang Daoists, and those of later centuries, adopted many typically Chinese ideas as their own. They also came to use Chinese ideas of how to organize a religion.

Long before the first Daoist texts were ever written, the Chinese wanted to hang on to life as long as they could. Symbols of long life—peaches, cranes, tortoises—decorated Chinese clothes, pottery, tools, instruments, houses—just about everything.

Confucianism, Buddhism, and Daoism are sometimes called the "three religions of China." This eighteenth-century painting shows the three patrons of those beliefs: (left to right) *Confucius, Buddha as a baby, and Lao-zi.*

Daoists first taught that following the Dao was an end in itself. It was its own reward. But after a while, the Daoists found that they could appeal to more people if they proposed that following the Dao could lead to immortality.

While other religions offer beliefs in an afterlife, Daoism became concerned with *how not to die in the first place.* Eventually a huge part of Daoist practice was devoted to formulas that would keep the body alive forever. Before immortality became the goal,

BIZARRE DAOIST PURSUITS

You could say they were the mad scientists of traditional China. For some Daoists the greatest goal was living forever. They believed their bodies could be preserved. Then they could take their place with the Shen-xian (shen-SHE-ahn), immortal beings with youthful bodies who lived in the wild places of the earth.

The trick, while you were still mortal, was to get rid of the "Three Worms and the Three Cadavers." The Daoists did all kinds of things to rid their bodies of these impurities. Some efforts were relatively tame. Men sunbathed to enhance their Yang, or their force of light and warmth. Women—who represented Yin, or darkness and coolness—exposed their bodies to the moon. Daoists also tried to mimic the "breathing" of fetuses in the womb. They thought this meant breathing as quietly and calmly as possible.

The craziest measures involved efforts to create a magic pill. Eating such a pill would make a person walk with the gods, they thought. The author of many recipes, a Daoist named Ko Hung, assured would-be immortals that his mixture "will immediately turn to gold." One pound (forty-five kilograms) of this gold will cure many illnesses and "make the Three Worms cry for mercy" in the body. If a person consumes 3 pounds (1.35 kilograms) of this gold, he or she will live "as long as nature itself."

Perhaps Ko Hung didn't realize that mercury, a common ingredient in such recipes, is deadly even in small amounts. A person who ate even 1 ounce (28 grams) of such a recipe would walk with the gods, but not as Ko Hung intended. Such a person would die, and many Daoists did perish searching for the magic formula for immortality.

Daoism was a fringe belief, a philosophy for misfits and rebels. After Daoism incorporated these notions of immortality, it became a potent force in mainstream Chinese society.

When Buddhism started to filter into China it brought a developed system of clergy, saints, and gods. It brought an organization. To compete with this new religion the once free-form Daoists started to develop an organization of their own. They did so in a typically Chinese fashion—the Daoist gods became organized in a heavenly bureaucracy.

As it turned out, the real-life bureaucracy had a direct impact on the heavenly one. During the Tang dynasty, Chinese rulers wanted to compete with Buddhism, a foreign religion, by strengthening native Chinese religions. The rulers started looking for a figure they could worship as the founder of the Daoist religion. Before, Lao-zi had been a legendary figure. But the Tang emperors started to teach that Lao-zi had been a man with the family name Li (lee) and the given name Er (ahr). Not by chance the Tang emperors also used the family name Li. If Li Er was the founder of Daoism, the emperors could claim to be related to him. Later they even started to say that Li Er had been one of Prince Siddhartha's teachers, so Buddhism really grew out of Daoism! Thus the Tang emperors took Daoism very seriously, and a new god, Li Er, took his position in the Daoist heavens.

The Buddha in China

The Tang emperors went to a great deal of trouble to prove that Buddhism also originated with their family. Their claim would strengthen their control over the many Chinese people who believed in Buddha's philosophy. Buddhism had great appeal. It made popular the ideas of mercy, charity, and hope. It influenced the arts of painting and sculpture. But many of Buddha's original ideas ran counter to common Chinese experience. For instance, Buddhism sees all men as essentially equal. Traditional Chinese society, with its ranks and rules, is essentially unequal. Although Buddhist gods and ideas were incorporated into popular culture, China changed Buddhism more than Buddhism changed China.

How Buddhism Changed

One of the reasons that Buddhism succeeded in China was that it readily accepted the Chinese teachings of Daoism and Confucianism. Gradually, the Chinese Buddhists accepted Daoist teachings as a lesser part of their religion. They also insisted that Buddhism did not conflict with the ideas of Confucius.

Actually, the ideas of Confucius altered Buddhism so much that it became almost a different faith in China. The historical Buddha, Prince Siddhartha, preached a philosophy in which men turned away from the world. Siddhartha had no gods in his vision. He said that each man must walk a solitary journey to enlightenment. Turning away from society, having no gods, being alone—to most Chinese these concepts were unthinkable. So the Chinese changed them.

The Chinese claimed that original Buddhism was the Smaller Vehicle, in which only a few made it to enlightenment. They flocked instead to another version of Buddhism from India, the Greater Vehicle. This form of Buddhism was better, they said, because it made Buddhism open to everyone. The Greater Vehicle offered a

This painting of a Buddhist guardian king is said to have been found in Turfan, in China's far west along the northern route of the Silk Road. It dates to the late Tang.

different set of truths: Instead of a godless universe, millions of gods exist in eons of time; instead of a solitary journey, ordinary people could depend on the saints, or bodhisattvas, to help them reach salvation; instead of relying on their own strength, they could rely on the strength of others—the bodhisattvas. Nirvana, the "snuffing out" of existence, came to mean never-ending existence in paradise.

In the end, however, these compromises to Chinese culture made Buddhism too strong for its own good. Chinese monasteries grew to be enormously influential. Some even had their own armies. Chinese emperors began to resent the vast lands held by monasteries that didn't pay taxes. They also disapproved of some Buddhists who taught that it was all right for monks to abandon their families.

PORTRAIT OF A BUDDHIST MONASTERY

During the Tang dynasty Buddhism reached the height of its prestige in China. Across the empire, giant Buddhist monasteries were built. Many housed thousands of monks and nuns. Every month or two, these religious institutions put on fairs and festivals that entertained the common people. Because early Tang emperors were devout Buddhists, the monasteries wielded power in the halls of the imperial court.

A visitor to one of these monasteries would see long processions of yellow-robed monks make their way through the courtyards, each monk fingering his prayer beads. These beads were used the way Roman Catholics use the rosary, counting off a bead for each prayer. Each day, services would be sung for the dead. They would take place in front of a great statue of Buddha, its face peaceful, one hand raised in blessing, the other pointed downward to symbolize giving.

In lecture halls near the temple, wise men and philosophers might spend the day in discussions. Hundreds of monks and laypeople labored in the kitchens and in the monastery gardens. The monks might operate a hospital for the sick and the poor. They operated inns, public baths, even banks.

By the end of the Tang dynasty most monasteries were so big and so powerful that they were like little empires within the greater Chinese empire. Finally, late Tang emperors decided the Buddhists were too rich and too mighty. They persecuted most of the monks and nuns in the monasteries and forced them to return to ordinary life.

Eventually the late Tang emperors took away the monasteries' lands. They forced the monks and nuns to return to their families. For the rest of Chinese history Buddhism faded into a sort of second-class status. Its much-humbled monasteries became refuges for society's outcasts. Of all its rituals only its funeral ceremonies continued to be observed by most Chinese.

Ideas and cultures can have a powerful influence on one another. In some cases an idea or a belief can create a basic change in a society. Confucianism did that in China. Society can also alter beliefs, as the Chinese altered Daoism to fit their needs. A civilization can also alter a philosophy beyond recognition. It can largely snuff out a religion. Both fates befell Buddhism in China. Often philosophers and religious teachers claim to have the only key to truth. In the land between the Yellow and the Yangtze Rivers, the Chinese seemed to know without being taught that reality involved a mixture of truths. Depending on the historical situation, they might add or take away pieces of one philosophy or the other—now a little more Buddhism or Daoism, then a heavy dose of Confucianism, perhaps a dash of superstition. The only constant was the constant mixture.

CHAPTER FIVE

THE DRAGON LIVES ON

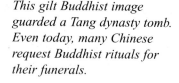

This gilt Buddhist image guarded a Tang dynasty tomb. Even today, many Chinese request Buddhist rituals for their funerals.

Frustrated history students often ask, "Why do I have to learn about all this stuff that happened hundreds, even thousands, of years ago?" Chinese culture is perhaps the best answer to this question. In today's China, up-to-date music videos, sing-along bars, discos, and fashion magazines thrive side by side with many, many bits of truly ancient beliefs and traditions.

Walking the streets of a modern city like Victoria in Hong Kong, Beijing in China, or Taipei in Taiwan, symbols created thousands of years ago still decorate billboards and advertisements. Little shrines honor gods and spirits that were worshiped a thousand years before Christ. Not only this, but the ideas of Confucius, Lao-zi, and Buddha still have very real power. The philosophies taught by these leaders not only influence people in China but also those who live in Korea, Japan, and in Southeast Asian countries like Vietnam, Thailand, and Singapore. In some cases these old, old ideas sway modern politics. They affect business. They even make a difference in the lives of children and teenagers—where their houses are built, whom they date, what they eat. Ancient Chinese tradition exists side by side with modern science and pop culture.

Symbols and Superstitions

The Little Things

In China, Hong Kong, and Taiwan the little things are probably the easiest to notice. Ancient symbols still abound. The calendars given out by real-estate agents and car dealers are decorated with peaches —the old sign for longevity—or with fish and peony flowers— signs for prosperity. In the back of most businesses—restaurants, small stores, laundries—stand small red shrines to local gods or to ancestors. In Tang times people lit candles before such altars.

Today they use electric bulbs that look like oversized Christmas lights. Otherwise, these little monuments haven't changed that much in thirteen hundred years. During holidays neon dragons ten or fifteen stories high hang on the outside of big office buildings in Hong Kong. Many bakers still decorate wedding cakes with the imperial symbols of the dragon and phoenix.

The wonders of modern science have not dimmed the Chinese enthusiasm for ghosts, soothsayers, fortune-tellers, and herbal medicine. The eaves of many Chinese buildings still turn up at the corners. When you walk into a Chinese restaurant, you often have to walk around a decorative wall. Why? Evil ghosts travel only in straight lines. The upturned roofs are supposed to send spirits flying far from the family courtyard. The walls that require a detour

The turned-up eaves of the Buddhist temple in southern China are pretty, but they have a "serious" purpose: Since ghosts travel only in straight lines, the eaves supposedly fling evil spirits far away.

63

FENG-SHUI

According to Chinese tradition, dragons live under every hill and mountain. In Tang times, people made sure that the dragons were in the appropriate places before they began constructing any building. To do this, they called an expert in *feng-shui* (pronounced "fung-schway"), which means "wind and water."

Using a special compass and charts of Yin and Yang, the Five Elements, the stars, and many other things, the *feng-shui* expert would make sure the building site was lucky. This could be very important, since people believed an unlucky siting of a grave could affect the descendants of a dead person.

In the best case, the Green Dragon of Spring should be on the left, and the White Tiger of Autumn should be on the right. If these two spirits are placed properly, they will protect the building, as if in the crook of an arm. This was only the beginning of the complex rules: Sites should be three-fifths Yang and two-fifths Yin; water should run by houses; winding roads are better than straight; trees and bamboo should be planted in flat, open areas.

If all this sounds silly, consider that many modern professionals and businesspeople in South China, Hong Kong, and Taiwan still consult *feng-shui* experts. *Feng-shui* is a profession like law or business. In California and New York, *feng-shui* specialists analyze some buildings before Chinese people will buy them. Some Chinese will rearrange their furniture to counteract bad *feng-shui*.

No one can *prove* that *feng-shui* works. But some stories seem to suggest there's something to it. The tallest building in the picture below—the Bank of China building with the dark triangles on the right—is supposed to have very bad *feng-shui*. Some believe it has cursed the governor's home, or "Government House," the low white building on the far right. Since the tower was built, the governor's daughter has had appendicitis, his dog ran away, and he was briefly hospitalized. Hong Kong Chinese say no governor has had good luck since the Bank of China tower went up.

Is it coincidence or bad *feng-shui*? No one is sure. But if you're planning to build anything soon, even a tree house, remember not to build it on the dragon's back!

block demons from entering restaurants. Just to be safe, some families also nail a small board across their stoop. People know to step over the barrier, but it's supposed to trip the ghosts.

Before making an important decision—like setting a wedding date or buying a house—many otherwise modern Chinese will consult some sort of fortune-teller. Or they may look for answers in the stars. When babies are born, Chinese grandmothers often rush to astrologers, who map the new child's prospects in accordance with ancient charts and the principles of the Five Elements. Still other people consult *feng-shui* (fung-shway), or "wind and water" experts, who tell them how to site their houses or rearrange their furniture to bring good luck.

Holidays

Even if they don't believe in such magic, the most skeptical resident of Canton or Shanghai participates in festivals that were celebrated by the Tang thirteen hundred years ago and by the Han almost a thousand years before that. The most famous of these celebrations is probably the New Year's holiday. The old lunar calendar, rather than our more modern solar calendar, determines the date. It usually falls in January or February.

In China the New Year celebration is like Thanksgiving, the Fourth of July, and Christmas rolled into one. A few days before, families make offerings to the Kitchen God. This deity judges people's behavior, much as Santa does in the West. The Kitchen God makes annual reports to the Jade Emperor. People lay out the choicest morsels in front of his altar in the hope that the god will say good things about them.

In very modern Taiwan, ancient local gods still command large followings. Here, a girl waits in front of a pig offered as a sacrifice at a folk temple.

The night before, people have a big dinner. They spend the whole evening making Chinese dumplings. In a manner similar to making ravioli, dough is folded in the shape of half-moons and filled with spiced meat. Families eat, drink, and talk until midnight. At the stroke of twelve the fun begins. In Hong Kong, the government puts on a huge fireworks display over the harbor. In Beijing,

65

On the Festival of the Dead, residents of Hong Kong pay respects to their ancestors. They burn incense and leave flowers and other offerings for them. Each rectangular space is a small cubicle that contains an urn with the ashes of the dead. Unlike mainland China, Hong Kong has few cemeteries because the island is small and rocky.

practically everyone rushes out into the street and lights firecrackers or small fireworks.

Just when things have settled down a little, people celebrate the Lantern Festival on the fourteenth, fifteenth, and sixteenth day of the New Year. The festival celebrates Buddha's birthday. Big businesses and organizations hang huge red silk lanterns in their gates. Families hang lanterns of all shapes and sizes in their windows and doorways. At night people crowd into parks to see hundreds of lanterns hung for contests. Almost every conceivable shape is constructed of silk and wood and lit from within: lanterns in the shape of dragons, lanterns that look like globes with space shuttles orbiting them, lanterns in the shape of political leaders and gods and cartoon characters.

About four months after the lanterns come down, families celebrate a more somber holiday: the Festival of the Dead. During Tang times the whole population left cities and towns to visit the graves of their ancestors in nearby hills. They swept clean the area around the graves, made offerings of food, and then stayed until dusk to enjoy the scenery. The Communist government of mainland China hasn't encouraged this practice, but many older people still celebrate this day of the dead. In Hong Kong, Taiwan, and Chinatowns around the world, the tradition remains very strong.

Traditional Medicine

In addition to symbols and holidays from the Tang dynasty, many Chinese with modern health plans still believe in traditional herbal medicines from ancient times. People return to the use of some drugs, like dried plants of various kinds, when Western cures don't seem to work. Rare substances, like rhinoceros horn, go into love potions. The Chinese demand for such rarities fuels some of the world's illegal trade in endangered species. In Taipei, the very modern capital of Taiwan, people still believe that snake blood is what makes a man a man. In the city's Snake Alley, vendors sell hooded cobras, vipers, green tree snakes, black snakes, and many other varieties for use in love potions and medicines.

Old Ideas, New Generations

The festivals, symbols, and beliefs from ancient times lend color and personality to modern Chinese culture. The arts of the Tang court—writing beautiful characters, composing poetry, and painting landscapes—are models for artists today. But the most profound legacy of the Tang is its mix of philosophy. The ideas of Lao-zi, Buddha, and Confucius still affect what goes on in the living rooms, the schools, and the offices of China.

The influence of Lao-zi and Buddha—of Daoism and Buddhism—is not as easy to identify as the longevity peaches in an advertisement for cold medicine. In the back alleys and small nooks of Chinese cities, people still light incense before shrines to Daoist gods. The physical disciplines of the Daoists live on as the kung fu and karate that are featured in movies and schools around the world. When they get old Chinese often become devoted to the ideas of Buddha and even enter Buddhist monasteries. Many Chinese ask that their families observe Buddhist funeral traditions when they die.

Traditional medicine shops like this one still thrive. Deer and antelope horns, used in love potions, lie on the counter. Such stores also sell monkey gallbladders, amber, freshwater pearls, ginseng root, and many other ingredients.

Eating Bitterness

Despite all these little details, Daoism and Buddhism have a larger effect on day-to-day life in another way: They have played an important role in molding what might be called the personality of the Chinese people. Though they differ on other points, both Daoism and Buddhism emphasize "going with the flow." Both Daoists and Buddhists think it is wise not to fight the natural order of things.

Over the centuries a great number of Chinese have thus come to accept a level of hardship that most Westerners would find intolerable. Commuting six hours a day, freezing in winter, studying until exhausted—the Chinese call this *chi ku* (chur koo). It means "eating bitterness." If they don't exactly like eating bitterness, the Chinese do admire a person's ability to do so. Suffering is the natural order of things.

Through most of history the Chinese people have not rebelled against their rulers until things got really, really bad. At the dawn of the twentieth century thousands upon thousands of Chinese were dying of starvation, robbers had made the roads unsafe, and people had little way to make a living. Meanwhile the emperor played tennis and ate delicacies in his palace. Only then did rebels overthrow the last imperial dynasty. Compare this with the United States, where colonists rebelled against England over a tax on tea and some notions of liberty.

This reluctance to make trouble doesn't mean the Chinese are passive. But if there's a problem most Chinese would rather find a way around it than fight it head on. For instance, a Chinese businessman might agree to something he doesn't really like and then just work around it. This is perfectly appropriate from the Chinese point of view. But peo-

A woman prays in a modern Daoist temple in present-day Hong Kong. People leave offerings on the tables before the altars. Sometimes, the round urns are filled with sand so that worshipers can put burning incense sticks in them.

ple from other cultures think it's unfair. This causes lots of misunder-standings in international business.

Confucius

The modern effects of Daoism and Buddhism are subtle, but the words of Confucius ring loud and clear in modern Chinese culture. Family, loyalty, and rank remain central to the way things are done in Beijing, Canton, Shanghai, and throughout the Chinese world. Chinese women do have more freedom today than at any time since the early Tang. They no longer bind their feet, they go to college, they work. But men still run Chinese society. Fathers and grand-fathers determine which children go to college, whether they may date, whether the family buys a new house. People are still admired for the respect they show their parents. The majority of children do not leave home until they marry. After their parents die, children continue to honor them as ancestors. When they decide to move abroad some people even dig up their ancestors and bring their remains to the new country.

The complicated government system that grew out of Confucian thought during the Tang dynasty still influences the way things are set up in China. Under Communist rule the names are different than they were in imperial China. But government is still a complex bureaucracy, a huge system of rankings and forms and rules that ultimately traces back to the system set up by Confucian scholar-officials of Tang times. Ultimate power still rests with the central government, as in Tang times.

What is more, Confucian ideals and systems, as well as Chinese culture, have filtered through to much of East Asia. This process began during Tang times. The Tang emperors conquered or influenced a truly enormous part of the world—from Japan and Korea in the northeast to Tibet and Vietnam in the west and south. Never before or since has such a large part of humanity looked to China as a role model.

Even after the Tang fell, Confucianism remained the domi-nant governing model for many societies. Chinese Confucian soci-ety became an ideal in Asia just as Greek democracy became an ideal for Western countries. During the Tang the rulers of Tibet, Korea, and Japan copied Chinese government down to the last

Imagine a character who's part Mickey Mouse, part Superman, part Bugs Bunny, and part Davy Crockett. Then perhaps you'd have a close copy of the hero of China's favorite fairy tale, *Xi You Ji* (she YO gee), which means "Journey to the West."

The novel, written three hundred years ago, combines Daoist, Buddhist, and ancient tales and builds on the legend of Xuan-cang. He was the pilgrim who brought back Buddhist scriptures from India during the Tang dynasty. But the hero of this tale is a magical character, known simply as Monkey.

Monkey first gets into trouble when he sneaks into the records of the King of the Dead and deletes the files of all the monkeys. Since there is no record in the underworld that they should die, they live forever. The Daoist god Lao-zi decides that Monkey needs to be kept out of mischief and sends him to watch over the orchard of the peaches of immortality. But Monkey proceeds to eat all the peaches. Not only this, he drinks up the whole supply of immortality potion. Now Lao-zi is really angry. He sentences Monkey to death. But Monkey has eaten so many immortality peaches and drunk so much immortality potion that not even Buddha can kill him. Buddha does manage to bury him under a mountain for five hundred years as punishment.

A Buddhist pilgrim comes upon this mountain and frees Monkey. Together Monkey and the pilgrim set out for India to get the Buddhist scriptures. Along the way they pick up two more companions—Pigsy, who is always eating, and Sandy, a mysterious being who had been haunting a river.

The group travels for fourteen years and has all sorts of adventures. They meet major and minor spirits, gods, demons, ogres, monsters, and fairies. Through all these episodes the pilgrim tries to keep everyone on track. But Pigsy always wants to eat, Sandy gets confused, and Monkey constantly gets into trouble, only to save everyone in the end.

The stories from this novel continue to be told today. Chinese cartoons feature the adventures of these characters. Monkey is pictured in television advertisements. At Chinese festivals people dressed up as Monkey, the pilgrim, Sandy, and Pigsy delight children, much as Mickey Mouse does at Disneyland.

In pictures, cartoons, and movies, Monkey is always leaping into action. In this painting he holds his trademark staff at the ready. Whenever he's in trouble, he twirls the staff around to defend himself.

detail—the examinations, the ministries, even the names of the offi-cials. As in China, strong leaders and fathers ruled those countries. Sacrifice for the good of the state was demanded.

This tradition has survived into the twentieth century. Fifty years ago, during World War II, Japanese pilots were so devoted to their emperor that they were willing to crash their planes into enemy ships. After World War II the common people of Korea ate mostly millet, a kind of grain porridge. Their sacrifice gave their government the freedom to spend money on building roads and shipyards and freeways. Korea became an economic powerhouse. The Tang emperors would have recognized and approved of these modern values: strong leadership, obedient citizenry, sacrifice, and prosperous economies.

Art and Literature

Tang art and literature still inspire people. In China and across East Asia people still tell stories about the "precious concubine" Yang Kui-fei and her "brilliant emperor." School-children memorize the poems of Li Po and Du Fu and memorize the same characters that Tang chil-dren did. Tang calligraphy has been admired and copied by scholars through the dynasties until the present. Artwork from the Tang is still treasured today. Glazed ceramics, tomb figurines, gold-ware and silverware are highly prized by museums and art collectors. It has been thirteen hundred years since Chang-an was a city of glory and the Tang emper-ors ruled much of East Asia. But in many ways the Tang dynasty is still very much alive.

In the modern art market, Tang ceramics are still very prized. This figure of a Central Asian merchant holding a wine pouch dates to the eighth century. Such "foreign" subjects were typical of Tang sophistication.

China and the Tang Dynasty: A Time Line

2000 B.C.E.

B.C.E.

2000 Xia dynasty (unverified), c. 2205–1766

Shang dynasty, c. 1766–1027

1000 **Western Zhou** dynasty, c. 1027–771

500 **Eastern Zhou** dynasty, c. 771-256

Qin dynasty, 221–207; capital: *Xian* (then called *Chang-an*)

200 **Han** (or **Former Han** or **Western Han**) dynasty, 202–9 C.E.; capital: *Xian* (then called *Chang-an*)

C.E.

10 **Xin** dynasty, 9–23; capital: *Xian* (then called *Chang-an*)

100 **Later Han** (or **Eastern Han**) dynasty, 25–220; capital: *Loyang*

200 Three Kingdoms era, 220–280

300 Qin (or Western Qin) dynasty, 266–316; capitals: *Loyang* to 311, then *Xian* (then called *Chang-an*)

Era of North–South division, 316–589

600 Sui dynasty, 581–618; capital: *Xian* (then called *Chang-an*)

TANG DYNASTY

600 **Tang** dynasty, 618–907; capital: *Xian* (then called *Chang-an*)

626: Emperor Tai-cong, "Grand Ancestor," comes to the throne

629: Buddhist monk Xuan-cang sets out for India

639–648: Emperor Tai-cong conquers kingdoms in West Asia, Tibet

645: Buddhist monk Xuan-cang returns to Chang-an with scriptures

649: Emperor Tai-cong dies

650

660: Wu Chao assumes control of government

690: Wu Chao declares herself empress

700

c. 700: Painter Wu Tao-zi born

701: Poet Li Po born

705: Empress Wu overthrown by a palace plot

712: Emperor Xuan-cang, "Brilliant Emperor," comes to the throne

Poet Du Fu born

C.E. **600 C.E.** **900 C.E.** **1900 C.E.**

750

751: Chinese armies disastrously defeated by Arabs at Talas; Tang power never fully recovers

755: An Lu-shan Rebellion

756: Emperor Xuan-cang dies

760: Painter Wu Tao-zi dies

762: Order restored to China after rebellion

763: Poet Li Po dies

770: Poet Du Fu dies

800

840–846: Emperor Wu-cung persecutes Buddhist monasteries

850

874: Northern uprisings against the Tang

900

907: Regional commander usurps the throne; Tang dynasty comes to an end

907–960 Five Dynasties era

1000 **Sung** (or **Northern Sung**) dynasty, 960-1127; capital: *Kaifeng*

Southern Sung dynasty, 1127–1279; capital: *Hangzhou*

Yuan dynasty, 1264–1368; Mongol rulers, capital: *Beijing*

1400 **Ming** dynasty, 1368–1644; capitals: *Nanjing* to 1421, then *Beijing*

1600

Qing dynasty, 1644–1912; Manchu rulers, capital: *Beijing*

1900 **Republic of China,** 1912–1949 on mainland; 1949–present in Taiwan; capitals: *Beijing* to 1927, *Nanjing* to 1949, then *Taipei*

People's Republic of China, 1949–present; capital: *Beijing*

The names in boldface are the major dynasties and governments in Chinese history. The italicized city names are the dynastic capitals. The names, unless otherwise indicated, are modern names.

73

GLOSSARY

acupuncture: the ancient practice of treating disease by inserting needles at precise points in the body

aristocrat: a member of the upper class

bureaucracy: a government divided into departments and divisions and managed by appointed officials who follow complex rules

calligraphy: beautiful handwriting; the art of writing this way

ceramics: the art of making nonmetallic-mineral articles, such as pottery

concubine: a woman who lives with a noble and has children by him but does not have the rights or position of a wife

culture: the ideas, customs, skills, and arts of a people

cursive: the art of writing in which the strokes of successive characters are joined and the angles rounded

Dao: "the Way"; according to some, the how, what, and why of everything

dragon: a mythical animal represented as a monstrous winged and scaly serpent

dynasty: a series of rulers who are members of the same family

eunuch: a castrated man who cares for the wives and concubines of a ruler

exotic: foreign, strange, different in a way that is fascinating

hierarchy: a group of persons or things arranged in order of rank

inkstone: a flat rock with a little bowl in one end used to prepare ink for writing

karma: the Indian Buddhist belief in a force generated by a person's good and bad actions that will determine one's place in the next life

kung fu: the art of self-defense

li: "Right Behavior"; the Confucian ideal of how to act

monopoly: exclusive possession or control of something

myth: a traditional story that explains the origin of things or the adventures of gods and heroes

nirvana: the Indian Buddhist belief in a place or state where one is oblivious to care and pain

patriarch: the father and ruler of a family or a tribe

phoenix: a legendary bird that lived five hundred years, burned itself to ashes, and then rose alive from the ashes

potent: having authority or power; mighty, influential

qi: literally, "breath"; soul, or the essence of being

ren: virtue, or a concern for other people

saltpeter: salt of a rock used in making gunpowder

symbol: something that stands for something else

FOR FURTHER READING

Chang, Monica. *Story of the Chinese Zodiac.* Taiwan: Yuan-Liou Pub., 1994.

Fabrian, Erika. *Costumes of Splendid China.* Taiwan: Getherease, 1994.

Hoobler, Dorothy, and Thomas Hoobler. *The Chinese-American Family Album.* Oxford and New York: Oxford University Press, 1994.

Hua, Long. *The Moon Maiden and Other Asian Folktales.* San Francisco: China Books, 1993.

Kalman, Bobbie. *China: The Culture.* New York: Crabtree, 1989.

Learning Tang Poetry. Guangzhou: China Record Co., 1994.

Stepanchuk, Carol. *Red Eggs and Dragon Boats—Celebrating Chinese Festivals.* Berkeley, California: Pacific View, 1993.

Wyndham, Robert. *Chinese Mother Goose Rhymes.* New York: Putnam's, 1989.

Yep, Lawrence. *The Rainbow People.* New York: Harper Trophy, 1989.

Yep, Lawrence. *The Star Fisher.* (fiction) New York: Puffin Books, 1992.

Yep, Lawrence. *Tongues of Jade.* New York: Harper Trophy, 1991.

Yu, Jin, and others. *Chinese Myths.* N.p.: Juvenile and Children's Pub. House, 1986.

CD-ROM: Chen, Ching-chih. *The First Emperor of China.* Irvington, N.Y.: Voyager, 1994.

Some of these books may be difficult to find. Many can be ordered from the catalog of China Books, San Francisco, California, (415) 282-2994.

BIBLIOGRAPHY

Birch, Cyril, ed. *Anthology of Chinese Literature.* New York: Grove Press, 1980.

Blunden, Caroline, and Mark Elvin. *A Cultural Atlas of China.* New York: Facts on File, 1983.

Chavannes, Edouard. *The Five Happinesses—Symbolism in Chinese Popular Art.* New York: John Weatherhill, 1953.

Christie, Anthony. *Chinese Mythology.* London: Feltham, Middlesex, Hamlyn, 1968.

DeBary, William Theodore et al. *Sources of Chinese Tradition,* Vol. I. New York: Columbia University Press, 1960.

Eberhard, Wolfram, ed. *Folktales of China.* Chicago: University of Chicago Press, 1965.

Ebrey, Patricia. *Confucianism and Family Rituals in Imperial China.* Princeton: Princeton University Press, 1991.

Fazzioli, Edouardo. *Chinese Calligraphy.* New York: Abbeville Press, 1987.

Fei, Hsiao-tung. *Peasant Life in China.* London: Routledge & Kegan Paul, 1939.

Gernet, Jacques. *Daily Life in China on the Eve of the Mongol Invasion.* Stanford: Stanford University Press, 1978.

Hucker, Charles O. *China's Imperial Past.* Stanford: Stanford University Press, 1978.

Hughes, E. R. *Religion in China.* London: Hutchinson's University Library, 1950.

Miyazaki, Ichisadu. *China's Examination Hell: The Civil Service Examination of Imperial China.* New Haven: Yale University Press, 1981.

Newnham, Richard. *About Chinese.* New York: Penguin, 1987.

Prodan, Mario. *An Introduction to Chinese Art.* London: Spring Books, 1958.

Reischauer, Edwin O., and John K. Fairbank. *East Asia: Tradition and Transformation.* Boston: Houghton Mifflin, 1973.

Ronan, Colin A., and Josephy Needham. *The Shorter Science and Civilization in China.* Oxford: Oxford University Press, 1994.

Schafer, Edward H. *The Golden Peaches of Samarkand: A Study of T'ang Exotics.* Berkeley, California: University of Southern California Press, 1967.

Schirokauer, Conrad. *A Brief History of Chinese and Japanese Civilizations.* New York: Harcourt, Brace, Jovanovich, 1978.

Treagar, Mary. *Chinese Art.* New York: Thames and Hudson, 1980.

Wu, Ch'eng-en (cq.). *Monkey.* New York, Grove Press, 1943.

INDEX

Page numbers for illustrations are in boldface

ABOUT THE AUTHOR

Heather Millar has long been fascinated with Chinese history and culture. She grew up in San Francisco and attended Stanford University, where she studied history and Chinese. After graduating from college, she spent eighteen months studying Chinese at Peking University in the People's Republic of China. While living overseas, she also worked for the *London Daily Telegraph* and traveled throughout China and Asia. She writes about China and current affairs for such publications as the *New York Times, Business Week,* and the *Atlantic Monthly.*

Ms. Millar lives in Manhattan with her husband, Peter, a newspaper editor, and her stepdaughter Maureen.